The Cherry Orchard

A Drama in Four Acts

by
Anton Chekhov

Translated by
Stark Young

D1510771

A SAMUEL FRENCH ACTING EDITION

SAMUEL FRENCH

FOUNDED 1830

SAMUELFRENCH.COM

THE CHERRY ORCHARD

(10 Males; 5 Females)

A Comedy in Four Acts

CHARACTERS

RANEVSKAYA, LYUBOFF ANDREYEVNA, *a landowner.*
ANYA, *her daughter, seventeen years old.*
VARYA, *her adopted daughter, twenty-four years old.*
GAYEFF, LEONID ANDREYEVITCH, *brother of Ranevskaya.*
LOPAHIN, YERMOLAY ALEXEYEVITCH, *a merchant.*
TROFIMOFF, PYOTOR SERGEYEVITCH, *a student.*
SEMYONOFF-PISHTCHIK, BORIS BORISOVITCH, *a landowner.*
CHARLOTTA IVANOVNA, *a governess.*
EPIHODOFF, SEMYON PANTELEYEVITCH, *a clerk.*
DUNYASHA, *a maid.*
FIERS, *a valet, an old man of eighty-seven.*
YASHA, *a young valet.*
A PASSERBY OR STRANGER.
THE STATION MASTER.
A POST-OFFICE CLERK.
VISITORS, SERVANTS.

The action takes place on the estate of L. A. Ranevskaya.

SYNOPSIS OF SCENES

ACT ONE
The nursery.

ACT TWO
A field.

ACT THREE
The drawing room.

ACT FOUR
Same as Act One.

STORY OF THE PLAY

"The Cherry Orchard" is now, and always has been, a play of inaction. It is crowded with pauses, sighs, chuckles and irrelevancies. There is incessant prattling by minor characters. There is somberness, sadness, gaiety and horseplay. It is still the story of a mortgage, with the grounds and beautiful trees of the proud landowners going to be sold at public auction to pay off their debts. Their estate gone, and sold to the boorish son of a peasant who has come along in industry, the family of Mme. Ranevsky—she is known as Lyubov Andreyevna in the present translation—depart to take up their lives anew, leaving the old and forgotten Fiers to die alone as the axes of the woodsmen are thudding ironically against the cherished trees.

CHEKHOV IN TRANSLATION

First of all I must acknowledge my indebtedness to Mrs. Catherine Alexander Burland. Without her close collaboration, her remarkable acquaintance with the two languages, and her great generosity, I could never have carried this translation of *The Cherry Orchard* through.

The one thing that a brief introduction of this sort may wisely attempt is to dispel at least a small part of the nonsense that exists among us about Chekhov. Thanks to Mrs. Garnett especially, and after her to various other translations, the impression of vagueness, moodiness, monotony of tone, even of incomprehensibility, that we have of Chekhov has sunk deep in stage tradition and in print. But we can at best try.

When my translation of *The Sea Gull* was produced by Mr. Alfred Lunt and Miss Lynn Fontanne, and presented by the Theatre Guild, the reception of the translation was generous indeed, the applause remarkable. And when the book was published, with an introduction on translating, there were reviews of it in some quarters as if it were a new successful novel. Nevertheless, there were plenty of people, critics and otherwise, who thought my version was brightened up, streamlined and abbreviated, or that something of the "Slavic mysticism" had been lost, of the famed Russian soul as it were, or even of a certain murky soul in general. As a matter of fact I followed the

ix

Chekhov text far more literally than did any one of the seven translations of the play I read.

To quote from my introduction to *The Sea Gull* (Scribner's), with regard to Chekhov:

"Our greatest surprise should be in the tone, which in a dramatic work is a diffused and intangible but final quality that reveals its general characteristic. A single page of his own text may be enough to show us now there has been gradually built up for Chekhov in English a tone quite false to him, so that our general conception of him is almost fantastically off the track. This is a great misfortune to our theatre. Chekhov has many qualities that we respond to, naturally and vividly. His technical method is one that we can not only admire but can make use of. He has already been a strong influence among us. He would be a much readier and deeper influence if his true tone could be established.

"We shall be surprised, too, at the number of contrivances in the writing itself, those balances, repetitions for stage effect, repetitions for stage economy, theatrical combinations and devices, time-patterns and so on, that are the fruits of much intention and technical craft, and that are almost totally absent from the translations—the truth is, if you went by the translations, you would never even suspect Chekhov of such practices.

"If the presence of these many contrivances surprised us, we should be even more surprised at the absence of a quality that most people have come to associate with Chekhov and that has done a good deal to set him back with the producers and darken his image with the public. I mean the impression of moodiness, monotony, vague-

ness, drab tone, even incomprehensibility that I have already mentioned. We seem to have accepted these traits
in *The Sea Gull*, traits tnat an otherwise admirable play
has to surmount. Or we admire their results as truly
Chekhovian; or welcome it as Slavic. That last is a fine
bit of tosh. Undoubtedly there are emotions, or combinations of emotions, and situations, in *The Sea Gull* that
might be called Slavic, but not the lines. The style in this
play is easy and clear, never confused or obscure so far
as the words themselves go. The structure of the sentences
could not be simpler. Fortunately we have a direct evidence on this point. 'How was one to utter these simplest
of phrases simply . . . ?' the directors at the new theatre
wondered. Stanislavsky, the régisseur in charge of *The
Sea Gull*, went even further: he did not, as he has told
us in writing, know any way at all to proceed; he found
the words too simple. So much, then, for our English
theatre and its tradition of Chekhov's moody vagueness."

To quote again: "I should have known all along that
Chekhov's lines would not be diffused or stuffy, studied,
elaborate or what not. His method, known as the realistic-
psychological, is to take actual material such as we find
in life and manage it in such a way that the inner mean-
ings are made to appear. On the surface the life in his
plays is natural, possible, and, in effect, at times even
casual. It should follow, therefore, that the words he
uses would be simple, or at least familiar or natural, as
we find them in our actual life day by day. The depths
and subtleties of meaning would, accordingly, not be
created by subtle words, difficult phrases, blurred clauses,
complex statements, vague lines, or a style of the muggy,

symbolic, swing-on-to-your-atmosphere sort. Not through such qualities in the words themselves, but through their management or combination would the inner content appear. But somehow I never suspected, from reading the translations, that fact." Note "the management or combination."

Mrs. Garnett's translations of Chekhov have been those most read and most used in the theatre. They steal a march on us. Such translating seems so sober, steady, painstaking and even, and conveys so unbroken an impression of scholarly care on the translator's part that we could never think of it as anything but accurate. If it sounds all mixed up, sounds intangible, we assume that the fault is Chekhov's. We could not be worse mistaken.

At the start I set myself as a translator a list of good intentions—shall we say of principles?—for all dramatic translation. The following are some of those that seemed in Chekhov's case more important.

To let Chekhov have his own way so far as possible. That is to say if he wants, for example, to reverse the word order, let him reverse it. If he wants to repeat a word, let him repeat it. On this second point, and on the first, for that matter, the translators in general are opposed. They evidently feel that Chekhov was too ignorant, or whatever it was, to know that you do not repeat the same word in the same sentence or passage. (Of course what Chekhov knew was that so far as life goes we constantly repeat the same word if the same urge is behind what we say, or if our ears are full of the word. And he knew that to change to another word merely to change the word, where the sense is the same, is merely

some school nonsense and a poor economy of style.)
Mrs. Garnett in particular always put Chekhov in his
place in this matter. For instance the last scene of *The
Sea Gull* has the tragic pistol shot ending the son's life; Dr.
Dorn, trying to soften matters, says he thinks a bottle of
ether has blown up, then goes out to see and returns to
say it is just as he thought, it blew up. Mrs. Garnett has
a change of words, once "blown up," once "exploded,"
which merely wastes our attention by making us wonder
what is the difference. There are endless cases of this
change of a word where Chekhov repeats it.

Well, for another point, to keep the language simple.
Nothing could be simpler than Chekhov's language. The
sublety appears in what is said and in the combinations
of simple remarks. We may save space by citing the
readiest evidence on this point, that of Stanislavsky,
which I have just quoted. In this matter of simplicity I
need only quote an extreme example in the reverse direc-
tion, from the Koteliansky translation of *The Sea Gull:*
"Your 'I' dissolves in you, and you already take yourself
for a third person—he." (What a scream that would be
read aloud on the stage!) It is, in fact, another way of
putting a very simple remark of the doctor's, which was
that Peter Nikolayevitch after a shot of vodka was himself plus another: "your ego splits up and you begin to
see yourself as another person."

There is no use stressing these absurdities, such, for
instance, as the Eismann translation, where the speech of
the young girl saying that she is drawn like a gull to this
lake, becomes "This ocean attracts me with invisible
power." As a matter of genuine obfuscation, I should cite

from Mrs. Garnett the speech about Nina and the young poet. "They are in love with each other and tonight their souls will be united in the effort to realize the same artistic effect." I recall that an intelligent actor confessed to me that he had rehearsed the scene many times and could never understand what these lines meant. This is not surprising, since the lines in spite of their implications could mean nothing at all. You cannot *realize* an *effect,* though you can realize a design carried out into some effect. The effect is the *realization;* the realization and the effect are the same thing. But Chekhov's word does not mean to realize anyhow. It means to "give," to "bestow on." And he does not say "artistic," he says "art," as in the phrase, "art theatre." He does not say in an effort, he says in a longing or aspiration. "The same" makes no sense at all; the same as what? All you have to do is to look up in the Russian dictionary what the words mean and you will see what Chekhov means and what makes sense in that passage. He merely says that these two are joined together in a longing to create one and the same thing in art—something that will be true to each of them and that both can share—which is a simple, moving dramatic idea.

Another translating principle I resolved on was to keep the speeches sayable—speakable—in the theatre. That means that the sense stresses coincide with the word stresses; it means that the emphasis will fall in the right place and will project the thought. It means also that the speech will be easy and natural, since Chekhov's method assumes a surface of the natural, and comes to us in an outer garment of the real or the natural.

For example there is a moment in *The Sea Gull* where, according to one translation, the manager of the place yells in a rage at the actress: "You don't know what the management of an estate involves," and where what Chekhov says is something that could really be shouted: "You don't know what farming means." The translations in general are full of speeches that no actor could put over. In fact Madame Ouspenskaya, who was the governess in *The Cherry Orchard* for many Russian years in the Moscow Art Theatre and gave one of the most remarkable performances I ever saw in the theatre, told me that, try as she might, she simply could not memorize or speak her lines as Mrs. Garnett had them in English.

I resolved also to keep the time values in the dialogue, since time is one of the chief elements in theatre dialogue, as much as the height of a tower is a part of it or the width of a table a part of the table. Which is to say— what an actor knows but the translators do not know— that a speech that takes twenty seconds to deliver is organically different, through its very time value, from a speech that takes forty seconds. It is, therefore, a manifold distortion to render a Chekhov speech "I am drawn to her" with "I am irresistibly impelled toward her," not to speak of the fussiness involved besides. Or when Chekhov says, "But what for?" to render it, "Though what his provocation may be I can't imagine." If these instances are rather unbelievable, I will subside with two ampler quotations. (The quotation is from *The Sea Gull* because that play is early, is in the more or less Ibsen tradition, is full of elaborate speeches, and thus invites the worst from the translators. They have made a kind of vague gloom its topmost flower.)

The actress' son in *The Sea Gull* says some remarkable things [I must confess that their confusion and energy made me first aware of Chekhov, silly as the translation is] : "I love my mother, I love her devotedly, but I think she leads a stupid life. She has always this man of letters on her mind, and the newspapers are always frightening her to death, and I am tired of it. . . . Personally I am nothing, nobody."

That was, as I have said, one of my first contacts with Chekhov and I remember how a kind of dramatic hysteria seized me at the thought of what astonishing people these Russians were and especially this young man, going on in that style. But now I know what Chekhov says. The young man merely says, "I love my mother—I love her very much—but she leads a senseless life, always making a fuss over this novelist [the Russian word is the same as for a woman making a fuss, for instance, over a poodle] her name forever being chucked about in the newspapers —it disgusts me . . . Who am I? What am I?" The difference here is a vast difference in impression. It is quite appalling in fact.

When the novelist says, "What success? I have never pleased myself. I don't like myself as a writer. The worst of it is I am in a sort of daze and often don't understand what I write . . . and the upshot is that I feel that I can write only landscape, and in all the rest I am false and false to the marrow of my bones," Mrs. Fell has it, "What success have I had? I have never pleased myself: as a writer I do not like myself at all. The trouble is that

I am made giddy, as it were, by the fumes of my brain, and often hardly know what I am writing . . . finally come to the conclusion that all I am fit for is to describe landscape and that whatever else I attempt rings abominably false."

The problem of translating *The Cherry Orchard* is in a way simpler than in some of the earlier plays. The great thing to seek is the flow and interchange of life by which our minds are engaged and our hearts are touched. Epihodoff is an uneducated man who speaks pompously and makes us wonder if the translation is wrong. Lopahin speaks like a peasant who has grown rich. But the great Chekhov qualities are there all through the play. A special characteristic of Chekhov is his wit. Underneath the play lies a pervading lyricism, a pressure that is intense and compelling; but the play as a whole is conceived within a frame of wit—Chekhov, a witty doctor who sees what human life is, what things in general are, how tragic, how confused and urgent they remain, but who keeps, nevertheless, a certain easy sense of humor, a poignant, smiling observation and scope. It is along this side that he sets down *The Cherry Orchard* as a comedy.

We should mention here that the Russians themselves have never ceased to be amazed at our audiences watching a Chekhov performance, wondering at the solemn, determined approach we maintain, the mood of soft gloom that we insist on, the monotony, the grey tone—like a dead cat—that we bring to this drama which to them is so lively, so vibrant, quivering and wholesome—not that they care whether it is wholesome or not—which is as it were a variant on the tragic life.

This attempt of mine, brief as it is, considering the subject, to clear matters up somewhat where Chekhov is concerned, will be of service, let us hope, to some of his public. To some it will not be. They will readily subside into the old entrenched conception of what Chekhov is like, just as there will always be those who believe what they heard in school, where they were told that it was Columbus who enlightened mankind as to the roundness of the earth, and this despite the fact that eleven years before Columbus sailed, Pope Pius II had begun a book with the truism that practically everybody agreed the earth is round—*Mundi formam omnes fere consentiunt rotundam esse*—and Aristotle taught it, and Parmenides a century before, and the great Alexander, whose tutor Aristotle was, marched eastward in that knowledge to conquer the world. We can only hope that in time Chekhov will be more simply and happily accepted among us, without all that accumulation of vague, obscurantist and contraceptive nonsense which has been foisted upon him, and that his delightful, sweet spirit, so exact, observant, poignant and human, will come to us and make us his, truly and inexhaustibly, happily, and at his full, deep, living content.

BIOGRAPHICAL NOTE

Anton Chekhov was born in Taganrog on January 17, 1860. He was of peasant stock, but his grandfather had bought the freedom of the family. Chekhov began writing at twenty, under the pen-name of Antosha Chekhonté. In the meantime, having taken his degree of Doctor of Medicine, he won a certain success for his writing when the Imperial Academy of Sciences awarded him the Pushkin Prize of five hundred rubles. From then on the mass of his writings steadily increased. Only his plays concern us here however.

The Swan Song, a one-act play, was written in 1886; *Ivanoff*, a play in four acts, was written in 1887 and produced at Korsh's Theatre and in St. Petersburg as well. *The Wood Demon*, a comedy in four acts, and the farces, *A Tragedian Against His Will* and *The Proposal*, came in 1889. By November 1895 he had finished *The Sea Gull* (the title is really *The Gull*, but that would make another sense in English) and that play was produced next year at the Alexandrinsky Theatre in St. Petersburg as part of an occasion in honor of an admired comedienne. This fact is not usually remembered, nor is the amount of perceptive praise recorded, in accounts of the sorry failure of that event. When it was produced next year by the new Moscow Art Theatre the play was an overwhelming success. It was, in fact, a furor. The failure and then the triumph of Chekhov's play is, therefore, as a rule rather foolishly played up in our theatre annals. The precise history here should, nevertheless, be recorded, which is that though there was this furor and ovation, the house was half empty, and the excitement did not imply any great popular acceptance of the play. The truth is that none of Chekhov's plays won any real triumph until its second season; and even after that it had to wait a long time before it drew large houses. We must add, too, that never in the entire history of Chekhov's plays, either in Russian or in translation abroad, did any Chekhov production, so far as I know, win such houses and such box-office as did the Alfred Lunt and Lynn Fontanne production of *The Sea Gull*.

In 1889 *Uncle Vanya* was produced by the Moscow Art Theatre. *The Three Sisters* came in 1901. *The Cherry Orchard* was finished in the autumn of 1903, and produced by the Moscow Art Theatre the following January. Chekhov meanwhile having tried for some years the softer climate of the Crimea, found his physical condition steadily worse. He died at Badenweiler, a German health resort, July 2, 1904, and was buried in Moscow. The freight car in which his body was brought to Moscow was marked "Oysters." Nobody would have been more entertained than Chekhov with the humor, pathos and human comedy of such a coincidence.

ACT ONE

ACT ONE

A room that is still called the nursery. One of the doors leads into ANYA'S *room. Dawn, the sun will soon be rising. It is May, the cherry trees are in blossom but in the orchard it is cold, with a morning frost. The windows in the room are closed. Enter* DUNYASHA *with a candle and* LOPAHIN *with a book in his hand.*

LOPAHIN. The train got in, thank God. What time is it?

DUNYASHA. It's nearly two. [*Blows out his candle.*] It's already daylight.

LOPAHIN. But how late was the train? Two hours at least. [*Yawning and stretching.*] I'm a fine one, I am, look what a fool thing I did! I drove here on purpose just to meet them at the station, and then all of a sudden I'd overslept myself! Fell asleep in my chair. How provoking!—You could have waked me up.

DUNYASHA. I thought you had gone. [*Listening.*] Listen, I think they are coming now.

LOPAHIN. [*Listening.*] No—No, there's the luggage and one thing and another. [*A pause.*] Lyuboff Andreyevna has been living abroad five years. I don't know what she is like now—She is a good woman. An easy-going, simple woman. I remember when I was a boy about fifteen, my father, who is at rest—in those days he ran a shop here in the village—hit me in the face with his fist, my nose

3

was bleeding.—We'd come to the yard together for something or other, and he was a little drunk. Lyuboff Andreyevna, I can see her now, still so young, so slim, led me to the wash-basin here in this very room, in the nursery. "Don't cry," she says, "little peasant, it will be well in time for your wedding"—[*A pause.*] Yes, little peasant—My father was a peasant truly, and here I am in a white waistcoat and yellow shoes. Like a pig rooting in a pastry shop—I've got this rich, lots of money, but if you really stop and think of it, I'm just a peasant— [*Turning the pages of a book.*] Here I was reading a book and didn't get a thing out of it. Reading and went to sleep. [*A pause.*]

DUNYASHA. And all night long the dogs were not asleep, they know their masters are coming.

LOPAHIN. What is it, Dunyasha, you're so——

DUNYASHA. My hands are shaking. I'm going to faint.

LOPAHIN. You're just so delicate, Dunyasha. And all dressed up like a lady, and your hair all done up! Mustn't do that. Must know your place.

[*Enter* EPIHODOFF, *with a bouquet: he wears a jacket and highly polished boots with a loud squeak. As he enters he drops the bouquet.*]

EPIHODOFF. [*Picking up the bouquet.*] Look, the gardener sent these, he says to put them in the dining room.

[*Giving the bouquet to* DUNYASHA.]

LOPAHIN. And bring me some kvass.

DUNYASHA. Yes, sir. [*Goes out.*]

EPIHODOFF. There is a morning frost now, three degrees of frost [*Sighing*] and the cherries all in bloom. I can not approve of our climate—I cannot. Our climate can never quite rise to the occasion. Listen, Yermolay Alexeyevitch, allow me to subtend, I bought myself, day before yesterday, some boots and they, I venture to assure you, squeak so that it is impossible. What could I grease them with?

LOPAHIN. Go on. You annoy me.

EPIHODOFF. Every day some misfortune happens to me. But I don't complain, I am used to it and I even smile.

[DUNYASHA *enters, serves* LOPAHIN *the kvass.*]

EPIHODOFF. I'm going. [*Stumbling over a chair and upsetting it.*] There [*As if triumphant*] there, you see, pardon the expression, a circumstance like that, among others.—It is simply quite remarkable. [*Goes out.*]

DUNYASHA. And I must tell you, Yermolay Alexeyevitch that Epihodoff has proposed to me.

LOPAHIN. Ah!

DUNYASHA. I don't know really what to— He is a quiet man but sometimes when he starts talking, you can't understand a thing he _neans. It's all very nice, and full of feeling, but just doesn't make any sense. I sort of like him. He loves me madly. He's a man that's unfortunate, every day there's something or other. They tease him around here, call him twenty-two misfortunes—

LOPAHIN. [*Cocking his ear.*] Listen, I think they are coming—

DUNYASHA. They are coming! But what's the matter with me—I'm cold all over.

LOPAHIN. They're really coming. Let's go meet them. Will she recognize me? It's five years we haven't seen each other.

DUNYASHA. [*Excitedly.*] I'm going to faint this very minute. Ah, I'm going to faint!

[*Two carriages can be heard driving up to the house.* LOPAHIN *and* DUNYASHA *hurry out. The stage is empty. In the adjoining rooms a noise begins.* FIERS *hurries across the stage, leaning on a stick; he has been to meet* LYUBOFF ANDREYEVNA, *and wears an old-fashioned livery and a high hat; he mutters something to himself, but you cannot understand a word of it. The noise off-stage gets louder and louder. A voice: "Look! Let's go through here—"* LYUBOFF ANDREYVNA, ANYA *and* CHARLOTTA IVANOVNA, *with a little dog on a chain, all of them dressed for travelling,* VARYA, *in a coat and kerchief,* GAYEFF, SEMYONOFF-PISHTCHIK, LOPAHIN, DUNYASHA, *with a bundle and an umbrella, servants with pieces of luggage —all pass through the room.*]

ANYA. Let's go through here. Mama, do you remember what room this is?

LYUBOFF ANDREYEVNA. [*Happily, through her tears.*] The nursery!

VARYA. How cold it is, my hands are stiff. [*To* LYUBOFF

ANDREYEVNA.] Your rooms, the white one and the violet, are just the same as ever, Mama.

LYUBOFF ANDREYEVNA. The nursery, my dear beautiful room—I slept here when I was little— [*Crying.*] And now I am like a child— [*Kisses her brother and* VARYA, *then her brother again.*] And Varya is just the same as ever, looks like a nun. And I knew Dunyasha— [*Kisses* DUNYASHA.]

GAYEFF. The train was two hours late. How's that? How's that for good management?

CHARLOTTA. [*To* PISHTCHIK.] My dog he eats nuts too.

PISHTCHIK. [*Astonished.*] Think of that!

[EVERYBODY *goes out except* ANYA *and* DUNYASHA.]

DUNYASHA. We waited so long— [*Taking off* ANYA'S *coat and hat.*]

ANYA. I didn't sleep all four nights on the way. And now I feel so chilly.

DUNYASHA. It was Lent when you left, there was some snow then, there was frost, and now? My darling [*Laughing and kissing her*], I waited so long for you, my joy, my life—I'm telling you now, I can't keep from it another minute.

ANYA. [*Wearily.*] There we go again—

DUNYASHA The clerk Epihodoff, proposed to me after Holy Week.

ANYA. You're always talking about the same thing—

[*Arranging her hair.*] I've lost all my hairpins— [*She is tired to the point of staggering.*]

DUNYASHA. I just don't know what to think. He loves me, loves me so!

ANYA. [*Looks in through her door, tenderly.*] My room, my windows, it's just as if I had never been away. I'm home! Tomorrow morning I'll get up, I'll run into the orchard— Oh, if I only could go to sleep! I haven't slept all the way, I was tormented by anxiety.

DUNYASHA. Day before yesterday, Pyotor Sergeyitch arrived.

ANYA. [*Joyfully.*] Petya!

DUNYASHA. He's asleep in the bathhouse, he lives there. I am afraid, he says, of being in the way. [*Taking her watch from her pocket and looking at it.*] Somebody ought to wake him up. It's only that Varvara Michailovna told us not to. Don't you wake him up, she said.

VARYA. [*Enter* VARYA *with a bunch of keys at her belt.*] Dunyasha, coffee, quick—Mama is asking for coffee.

DUNYASHA. This minute. [*Goes out.*]

VARYA. Well, thank goodness, you've come back. You are home again. [*Caressingly.*] My darling is back! My precious is back!

ANYA. I've had such a time.

VARYA. I can imagine!

ANYA. I left during Holy Week, it was cold then. Charlotta talked all the way and did her tricks. Why did you fasten Charlotta on to me—?

VARYA. But you couldn't have travelled alone, darling; not at seventeen!

ANYA. We arrived in Paris, it was cold there and snowing. I speak terrible French. Mama lived on the fifth floor; I went to see her; there were some French people in her room, ladies, an old priest with his prayer book, and the place was full of tobacco smoke—very dreary. Suddenly I began to feel sorry for Mama, so sorry, I drew her to me, held her close and couldn't let her go. Then Mama kept hugging me, crying—yes—

VARYA. [*Tearfully.*] Don't—oh, don't—

ANYA. Her villa near Mentone she had already sold, she had nothing left, nothing. And I didn't have a kopeck left. It was all we could do to get here. And Mama doesn't understand! We sit down to dinner at a station and she orders, insists on the most expensive things and gives the waiters rouble tips. Charlotta does the same. Yasha too demands his share; it's simply dreadful. Mama has her butler, Yasha, we've brought him here—

VARYA. I saw the wretch.

ANYA. Well, how are things? Has the interest on the mortgage been paid?

VARYA. How could we?

ANYA. Oh, my God, my God—!

VARYA. In August the estate is to be sold—

ANYA. My God—!

LOPAHIN. [*Looking in through the door and mooing like a cow.*] Moo-o-o— [*Goes away.*]

VARYA. [*Tearfully.*] I'd land him one like that— [*Shaking her fist.*]

ANYA. [*Embracing* VARYA *gently.*] Varya, has he proposed? [VARYA *shakes her head.*] But he loves you— Why don't you have it out with him, what are you waiting for? VARYA. I don't think anything will come of it for us. He is very busy, he hasn't any time for me—And doesn't notice me. God knows, it's painful for me to see him— Everybody talks about our marriage, everybody congratulates us, and the truth is, there's nothing to it—it's all like a dream— [*In a different tone.*] You have a brooch looks like a bee.

ANYA. [*Sadly.*] Mama bought it. [*Going toward her room, speaking gaily, like a child.*] And in Paris I went up in a balloon!

VARYA. My darling is back! My precious is back! [DUN-YASHA *has returned with the coffee pot and is making coffee.* VARYA *is standing by the door.*] Darling, I'm busy all day long with the house and I go around thinking things. If only you could be married to a rich man, I'd be more at peace too, I would go all by myself to a hermitage—then to Kieff—to Moscow, and I'd keep going like that from one holy place to another—I would go on and on. Heavenly!

ANYA. The birds are singing in the orchard. What time is it now?

VARYA. It must be after two. It's time you were asleep, darling. [*Going into* ANYA'S *room.*] Heavenly!

YASHA. [YASHA *enters with a lap-robe and a travelling bag. Crossing the stage airily.*] May I go through here?

DUNYASHA. We'd hardly recognize you, Yasha; you've changed so abroad!

YASHA. Hm— And who are you?

DUNYASHA. When you left here, I was like that— [*Her hand so high from the floor.*] I'm Dunyasha, Fyodor Kozoyedoff's daughter. You don't remember!

YASHA. Hm— You little peach!

[*Looking around before he embraces her; she shrieks and drops a saucer,* YASHA *hurries out.*]

VARYA. [*At the door, in a vexed tone.*] And what's going on here?

DUNYASHA. [*Tearfully.*] I broke a saucer—

VARYA. That's good luck.

ANYA. [*Emerging from her room.*] We ought to tell Mama beforehand: Petya is here—

VARYA. I told them not to wake him up.

ANYA. [*Pensively.*] Six years ago our father died, a month later our brother Grisha was drowned in the river, such a pretty little boy, just seven. Mama couldn't bear it, she went away, went away without ever looking back— [*Shuddering.*] How I understand her, if she only knew

I did. [*A pause.*] And Petya Trofimoff was Grisha's tutor, he might remind—

FIERS. [*Enter* FIERS; *he is in a jacket and white waist-coat. Going to the coffee urn, busy with it.*] The mistress will have her breakfast here— [*Putting on white gloves.*] Is the coffee ready? [*To* DUNYASHA, *sternly.*] You! What about the cream?

DUNYASHA. Oh, my God— [*Hurrying out.*]

FIERS. [*Busy at the coffee urn.*] Oh, you good-for-nothing—! [*Muttering to himself.*] Come back from Paris— And the master used to go to Paris by coach— [*Laughing.*]

VARYA. Fiers, what are you—?

FIERS. At your service. [*Joyfully.*] My mistress is back! It's what I've been waiting for! Now I'm ready to die— [*Crying for joy.*]

[LYUBOFF ANDREYEVNA, GAYEFF *and* SEMYONOFF PISH-TCHIK *enter;* SEMYONOFF-PISHTCHIK *is in a podyovka of fine cloth and sharovary.* GAYEFF *enters; he makes gestures with his hands and body as if he were playing billiards.*]

LYUBOFF ANDREYEVNA. How is it? Let me remember— Yellow into the corner! Duplicate in the middle!

GAYEFF. I cut into the corner. Sister, you and I slept here in this very room once, and now I am fifty-one years old, strange as that may seem—

LOPAHIN. Yes, time passes.

GAYEFF. What?

LOPAHIN. Time, I say, passes.

GAYEFF. And it smells like patchouli here.

ANYA. I'm going to bed. Good night, Mama. [*Kissing her mother.*]

LYUBOFF ANDREYEVNA. My sweet little child. [*Kissing her hands.*] You're glad you are home? I still can't get myself together.

ANYA. Good-bye, Uncle.

GAYEFF. [*Kissing her face and hands.*] God be with you. How like your mother you are! [*To his sister.*] Lyuba, at her age you were exactly like her.

[ANYA *shakes hands with* LOPAHIN *and* PISHTCHIK, *goes out and closes the door behind her.*]

LYUBOFF ANDREYEVNA. She's very tired.

PISHTCHIK. It is a long trip, I imagine.

VARYA. [*To* LOPAHIN *and* PISHTCHIK.] Well, then, Sirs? It's going on three o'clock, time for gentlemen to be going.
LYUBOFF ANDREYEVNA. [*Laughing.*] The same old Varya. [*Drawing her to her and kissing her.*] There, I'll drink my coffee, then we'll all go. [FIERS *puts a small cushion under her feet.*] Thank you, my dear. I am used to coffee. Drink it day and night. Thank you, my dear old soul.

[*Kissing* FIERS.]

VARYA. I'll go see if all the things have come. [*Goes out.*]

LYUBOFF ANDREYEVNA. Is it really me sitting here?
[*Laughing.*] I'd like to jump around and wave my arms.
[*Covering her face with her hands.*] But I may be dreaming! God knows I love my country, love it deeply, I
couldn't look out of the car window, I just kept crying.
[*Tearfully.*] However, I must drink my coffee. Thank
you, Fiers, thank you, my dear old friend. I'm so glad
you're still alive.

FIERS. Day before yesterday.

GAYEFF. He doesn't hear well.

LOPAHIN. And I must leave right now. It's nearly five
o'clock in the morning, for Kharkoff. What a nuisance!
I wanted to look at you—talk— You are as beautiful as
ever.

PISHTCHIK. [*Breathing heavily.*] Even more beautiful—
In your Paris clothes— It's a feast for the eyes—

LOPAHIN. Your brother, Leonid Andreyevitch here, says
I'm a boor, a peasant money grubber, but that's all the
same to me, absolutely. Let him say it. All I wish is you'd
trust me as you used to, and your wonderful, touching
eyes would look at me as they did. Merciful God! My
father was a serf; belonged to your grandfather and your
father; but you, your own self, you did so much for me
once that I've forgotten all that and love you like my
own kin—more than my kin.

LYUBOFF ANDREYEVNA. I can't sit still—I can't. [*Jumping
up and walking about in great excitement.*] I'll never live
through this happiness— Laugh at me, I'm silly— My own

little bookcase—! [*Kissing the bookcase.*] My little table!

GAYEFF. And in your absence the nurse here died.

LYUBOFF ANDREYEVNA. [*Sitting down and drinking coffee.*] Yes, may she rest in Heaven! They wrote me.

GAYEFF. And Anastasy died. Crossed-eyed Petrushka left me and lives in town now at the police officer's. [*Taking out of his pocket a box of hard candy and sucking a piece.*]

PISHTCHIK. My daughter, Dashenka—sends you her greetings—

LOPAHIN. I want to tell you something very pleasant, cheerful. [*Glancing at his watch.*] I'm going right away. There's no time for talking. Well, I'll make it two or three words. As you know, your cherry orchard is to be sold for your debts; the auction is set for August 22nd, but don't you worry, my dear, you just sleep in peace, there's a way out of it. Here's my plan. Please listen to me. Your estate is only thirteen miles from town. They've run the railroad by it. Now if the cherry orchard and the land along the river were cut up into building lots and leased for summer cottages, you'd have at the very lowest twenty-five thousand roubles per year income.

GAYEFF. Excuse me, what rot!

LYUBOFF ANDREYEVNA. I don't quite understand you, Yermolay Alexeyevitch.

LOPAHIN. At the very least you will get from the summer residents twenty-five roubles per year for a two-and-a-half acre lot and if you post a notice right off, I'll bet you anything that by autumn you won't have a single patch of land free, everything will be taken. In a word, my congratulations, you are saved. The location is wonderful, the river's so deep. Except, of course, it all needs to be tidied up, cleared— For instance, let's say, tear all the old buildings down and this house, which is no good any more, and cut down the old cherry orchard—

LYUBOFF ANDREYEVNA. Cut down? My dear, forgive me, you don't understand at all. If there's one thing in the whole province that's interesting—not to say remarkable—it's our cherry orchard.

LOPAHIN. The only remarkable thing about this cherry orchard is that it's very big. There's a crop of cherries once every two years and even that's hard to get rid of. Nobody buys them.

GAYEFF. This orchard is even mentioned in the encyclopedia.

LOPAHIN. [*Glancing at his watch.*] If we don't cook up something and don't get somewhere, the cherry orchard and the entire estate will be sold at auction on the twenty-second of August. Do get it settled then! I swear there is no other way out. Not a one!

FIERS. There was a time, forty-fifty years ago when the cherries were dried, soaked, pickled, cooked into jam and it used to be—

GAYEFF. Keep quiet, Fiers.

FIERS. And it used to be that the dried cherries were shipped by the wagon-load to Moscow and to Kharkoff.

And the money there was! And the dried cherries were soft then, juicy, sweet, fragrant— They had a way of treating them then—

LYUBOFF ANDREYEVNA. And where is that way now?

FIERS. They have forgotten it. Nobody remembers it.

PISHTCHIK. [*To* LYUBOFF ANDREYEVNA.] What's happening in Paris? How is everything? Did you eat frogs?

LYUBOFF ANDREYEVNA. I ate crocodiles.

PISHTCHIK. Think of it—!

LOPAHIN. Up to now in the country there have been only the gentry and the peasants, but now in summer the villa people too are coming in. All the towns, even the least big ones, are surrounded with cottages. In about twenty years very likely the summer resident will multiply enormously. He merely drinks tea on the porch now, but it might well happen that on this two-and-a-half acre lot of his, he'll go in for farming, and then your cherry orchard would be happy, rich, splendid—

GAYEFF. [*Getting hot.*] What rot!

[*Enter* VARYA *and* YASHA.]

VARYA. Here, Mama. Two telegrams for you. [*Choosing a key and opening the old bookcase noisily.*] Here they are.

LYUBOFF ANDREYEVNA. From Paris. [*Tearing up the telegrams without reading them.*] Paris, that's all over—

GAYEFF. Do you know how old this bookcase is, Lyuba?

A week ago I pulled out the bottom drawer and looked, and there the figures were burned on it. The bookcase was made exactly a hundred years ago. How's that? Eh? You might celebrate its jubilee. It's an inanimate object, but all the same, be that as it may, it's a bookcase.

PISHTCHIK. [*In astonishment.*] A hundred years—! Think of it—!

GAYEFF. Yes—quite something— [*Shaking the bookcase.*] Dear, honored bookcase! I salute your existence, which for more than a hundred years has been directed toward the clear ideals of goodness and justice; your silent appeal to fruitful endeavor has not flagged in all the course of a hundred years, sustaining [*tearfully*] through the generations of our family, our courage and our faith in a better future and nurturing in us ideals of goodness and of a social consciousness.

[*A pause.*]

LOPAHIN. Yes.

LYUBOFF ANDREYEVNA. You're the same as ever, Lenya.
GAYEFF. [*Slightly embarrassed.*] Carom to the right into the corner pocket. I cut into the side pocket!

LOPAHIN. [*Glancing at his watch.*] Well, it's time for me to go.

YASHA. [*Handing medicine to* LYUBOFF ANDREYEVNA.] Perhaps you'll take the pills now—

PISHTCHIK. You should never take medicaments, dear madam— They do neither harm nor good— Hand them here, dearest lady. [*He takes the pill box, shakes the pills out into his palm, blows on them, puts them in his mouth and washes them down with kvass.*] There! Now!

LYUBOFF ANDREYEVNA. [*Startled.*] Why, you've lost your mind!

PISHTCHIK. I took all the pills.

LOPAHIN. Such a glutton!

[EVERYONE *laughs.*]

FIERS. The gentleman stayed with us during Holy Week, he ate half a bucket of pickles— [*Muttering.*]

LYUBOFF ANDREYEVNA. What is he muttering about?

VARYA. He's been muttering like that for three years. We're used to it.

YASHA. In his dotage.

[CHARLOTTA IVANOVNA *in a white dress—she is very thin, her corset laced very tight—with a lorgnette at her belt, crosses the stage.*]

LOPAHIN. Excuse me, Charlotta Ivanovna, I haven't had a chance yet to welcome you. [*Trying to kiss her hand.*]

CHARLOTTA. [*Drawing her hand away.*] If I let you kiss my hand, 'twould be my elbow next, then my shoulder—
LOPAHIN. No luck for me today. [EVERYONE *laughs.*]

Charlotta Ivanovna, show us a trick!

CHARLOTTA. No. I want to go to bed. [*Exit.*]

LOPAHIN. In three weeks we shall see each other. [*Kissing* LYUBOFF ANDREYEVNA'S *hand.*] Till then, good-bye. It's time. [*To* GAYEFF.] See you soon. [*Kissing* PISHTCHIK.] See you soon. [*Shaking* VARYA'S *hand, then* FIERS' *and* YASHA'S.] I don't feel like going. [*To* LYUBOFF ANDREYEVNA.] If you think it over and make up your mind about the summer cottages, let me know and I'll arrange a loan of something like fifty thousand roubles. Think it over seriously.

VARYA. [*Angrily.*] Do go on, anyhow, will you!

LOPAHIN. I'm going, I'm going— [*Exit.*]

GAYEFF. Boor. However, pardon—Varya is going to marry him, it's Varya's little fiancé.

VARYA. Don't talk too much, Uncle.

LYUBOFF ANDREYEVNA. Well, Varya, I should be very glad. He's a good man.

PISHTCHIK. A man, one must say truthfully—A most worthy—And my Dashenka—says also that—she says all sorts of things— [*Snoring but immediately waking up.*] Nevertheless, dearest lady, oblige me—With a loan of two hundred and forty roubles— Tomorrow the interest on my mortgage has got to be paid—

VARYA. [*Startled.*] There's not any money, none at all.

LYUBOFF ANDREYEVNA. Really, I haven't got anything.

PISHTCHIK. I'll find it, somehow. [*Laughing.*] I never give up hope. There, I think to myself, all is lost, I am ruined and lo and behold—a railroad is put through my land and—they paid me. And then, just watch, something else will turn up—if not today, then tomorrow—Dashenka will win two hundred thousand— She has a ticket.

LYUBOFF ANDREYEVNA. We've finished the coffee, now we can go to bed.

FIERS. [*Brushing* GAYEFF'S *clothes, reprovingly.*] You put on the wrong trousers again. What am I going to do with you!

VARYA. [*Softly.*] Anya is asleep. [*Opening the window softly.*] Already the sun's rising—it's not cold. Look, Mama! What beautiful trees! My Lord, what air! The starlings are singing!

GAYEFF. [*Opening another window.*] The orchard is all white. You haven't forgotten, Lyuba? That long lane there runs straight—as a strap stretched out. It glistens on moonlight nights. Do you remember? You haven't forgotten it?

LYUBOFF ANDREYEVNA. [*Looking out of the window on to the orchard.*] Oh, my childhood, my innocence! I slept in this nursery and looked out on the orchard from here, every morning happiness awoke with me, it was just as it is now, then, nothing has changed. [*Laughing with joy.*] All, all white! Oh, my orchard! After a dark, rainy autumn and cold winter, you are young again and full of happiness. The heavenly angels have not deserted you. —If I only could lift the weight from my breast, from my shoulders, if I could only forget my past!

GAYEFF. Yes, and the orchard will be sold for debt, strange as that may seem.

LYUBOFF ANDREYEVNA. Look, our dear Mother is walking through the orchard—In a white dress! [*Laughing happily.*] It's she.

GAYEFF. Where?

VARYA. God be with you, Mama!

LYUBOFF ANDREYEVNA. There's not anybody, it only seemed so. To the right, as you turn to the summer-house, a little white tree is leaning there, looks like a woman— [*Enter* TROFIMOFF, *in a student's uniform, well worn, and glasses.*] What a wonderful orchard! The white masses of blossoms, the sky all blue.

TROFIMOFF. Lyuboff Andreyevna! [*She looks around at him.*] I will just greet you and go immediately. [*Kissing her hand warmly.*] I was told to wait until morning, but I hadn't the patience—

[LYUBOFF ANDREYEVNA *looks at him puzzled.*]

VARYA. [*Tearfully.*] This is Petya Trofimoff—

TROFIMOFF. Petya Trofimoff, the former tutor of your Grisha— Have I really changed so?

[LYUBOFF ANDREYEVNA *embraces him; and crying quietly.*]

GAYEFF. [*Embarrassed.*] There, there, Lyuba.

VARYA. [*Crying.*] I told you, Petya, to wait till tomorrow.

LYUBOFF ANDREYEVNA. My Grisha—My boy—Grisha—Son—

VARYA. What can we do, Mama? It's God's will.

TROFIMOFF. [*In a low voice tearfully.*] There, there—

LYUBOFF ANDREYEVNA. [*Weeping softly.*] My boy was lost, drowned— Why? Why, my friend? [*More quietly.*] Anya is asleep there, and I am talking so loud—Making so much noise— But why, Petya? Why have you lost your looks? Why do you look so much older?

TROFIMOFF. A peasant woman on the train called me a mangy-looking gentleman.

LYUBOFF ANDREYEVNA. You were a mere boy then, a charming young student, and now your hair's not very thick any more and you wear glasses. Are you really a student still? [*Going to the door.*]

TROFIMOFF. Very likely I'll be a perennial student.

LYUBOFF ANDREYEVNA. [*Kissing her brother, then* VARYA.] Well, go to bed— You've grown older too, Leonid.

PISHTCHIK. [*Following her.*] So that's it, we are going to bed now. Oh, my gout! I'm staying here— I'd like, Lyuboff Andreyevna, my soul, tomorrow morning—Two hundred and forty roubles—

GAYEFF. He's still at it.

PISHTCHIK. Two hundred and forty roubles—To pay interest on the mortgage.

LYUBOFF ANDREYEVNA. I haven't any money, my dove.

PISHTCHIK. I'll pay it back, my dear— It's a trifling sum—

LYUBOFF ANDREYEVNA. Oh, very well, Leonid will give— You give it to him, Leonid.

GAYEFF. Oh, certainly, I'll give it to him. Hold out your pockets.

LYUBOFF ANDREYEVNA. What can we do, give it, he needs it— He'll pay it back.

[LYUBOFF ANDREYEVNA, TROFIMOFF, PISHTCHIK *and* FIERS *go out.* GAYEFF, VARYA *and* YASHA *remain.*]

GAYEFF. My sister hasn't yet lost her habit of throwing money away. [*To* YASHA.] Get away, my good fellow, you smell like hens.

YASHA. [*With a grin.*] And you are just the same as you used to be, Leonid Andreyevitch.

GAYEFF. What? [*To* VARYA.] What did he say?

VARYA. [*To* YASHA.] Your mother has come from the village, she's been sitting in the servants' hall ever since yesterday, she wants to see you—

YASHA. The devil take her!

VARYA. Ach, shameless creature!

YASHA. A lot I need her! She might have come tomorrow.

[*Goes out.*]

VARYA. Mama is just the same as she was, she hasn't changed at all. If she could, she'd give away everything she has.

GAYEFF. Yes— If many remedies are prescribed for an illness, you may know the illness is incurable. I keep thinking, I wrack my brains, I have many remedies, a great many, and that means, really, I haven't any at all. It would be fine to inherit a fortune from somebody, it would be fine to marry off our Anya to a very rich man, it would be fine to go to Yaroslavl and try our luck with our Aunt, the Countess. Auntie is very, very rich.

VARYA. [*Crying.*] If God would only help us!

GAYEFF. Don't bawl! Auntie is very rich but she doesn't like us. To begin with, Sister married a lawyer, not a nobleman— [ANYA *appears at the door.*] Married not a nobleman and behaved herself, you could say, not very virtuously. She is good, kind, nice, I love her very much, but no matter how much you allow for the extenuating circumstances, you must admit she's a depraved woman. You feel it in her slightest movement.

VARYA. [*Whispering.*] Anya is standing in the door there.

GAYEFF. What? [*A pause.*] It's amazing, something got in my right eye. I am beginning to see poorly. And on Thursday, when I was in the District Court—

[ANYA *enters.*]

VARYA. But why aren't you asleep, Anya?

ANYA. I don't feel like sleeping. I can't.

GAYEFF. My little girl— [*Kissing* ANYA's *face and hands.*] My child— [*Tearfully.*] You are not my niece, you are my angel, you are everything to me. Believe me, believe—

ANYA. I believe you, Uncle. Everybody loves you, respects you— But dear Uncle, you must keep quiet, just keep quiet— What were you saying, just now, about my mother, about your own sister? What did you say that for?

GAYEFF. Yes, yes— [*Putting her hand up over his face.*] Really, it's terrible! My God! O, God, save me! And today I made a speech to the bookcase— So silly! And it was only when I finished it that I could see it was silly.

VARYA. It's true, Uncle, you ought to keep quiet. Just keep quiet. That's all.

ANYA. If you kept quiet, you'd have more peace.

GAYEFF. I'll keep quiet. [*Kissing* ANYA's *and* VARYA's *hands.*] I'll keep quiet. Only this, it's about business. On Thursday I was in the District Court; well, a few of us gathered around and a conversation began about this and that, about lots of things; apparently it will be possible to arrange a loan on a promissory note to pay the bank the interest due.

VARYA. If the Lord would only help us!

GAYEFF. Tuesday I shall go and talk it over again. [*To* VARYA.] Don't bawl! [*To* ANYA.] Your mother will talk to Lopahin; of course, he won't refuse her— And as soon as you rest up, you will go to Yaroslavl to your grandmother, the Countess. There, that's how we will move from three directions, and the business is in the bag. We'll pay the interest. I am convinced of that— [*Putting a hard candy in his mouth.*] On my honor I'll swear, by anything you like, that the estate shall not be sold! [*Excitedly.*] By my happiness, I swear! Here's my hand, call me a worthless, dishonorable man, if I allow it to come up for auction! With all my soul I swear it!

ANYA. [*A quieter mood returns to her; she is happy.*] How good you are, Uncle, how clever! [*Embracing her uncle.*] I feel easy now! I feel easy! I'm happy!

FIERS. [FIERS *enters, reproachfully.*] Leonid Andreyevitch, have you no fear of God! When are you going to bed?

GAYEFF. Right away, right away. You may go, Fiers. For this once I'll undress myself. Well, children, beddy bye— More details tomorrow, and now, go to bed. [*Kissing* ANYA *and* VARYA.] I am a man of the eighties— It is a period that's not admired, but I can say, nevertheless, that I've suffered no little for my convictions in the course of my life. It is not for nothing that the peasant loves me. One must know the peasant! One must know from what—

ANYA. Again, Uncle!

VARYA. You, Uncle dear, keep quiet.

FIERS. [*Angrily.*] Leonid Andreyevitch!

GAYEFF. I'm coming, I'm coming— Go to bed. A double bank into the side pocket! A clean shot—

[*Goes out,* FIERS *hobbling after him.*]

ANYA. I feel easy now. I don't feel like going to Yaroslavl; I don't like grandmother, but still I feel easy. Thanks to Uncle. [*Sits down.*]

VARYA. I must get to sleep. I'm going. And there was un-

pleasantness here during your absence. In the old servants' quarters, as you know, live only the old servants:
Yephemushka, Polya, Yevstignay, well, and Karp. They
began to let every sort of creature spend the night with
them—I didn't say anything. But then I hear they've
spread the rumor that I'd given orders to feed them nothing but beans. Out of stinginess, you see— And all that
from Yevstignay— Very well, I think to myself. If that's
the way it is, I think to myself, then you just wait. I call
in Yevstignay— [*Yawning.*] He comes— How is it, I say,
that you, Yevstignay— You're such a fool— [*Glancing at*
ANYA.] Anitchka!—[*A pause.*] Asleep! [*Takes* ANYA *by
her arm.*] Let's go to bed— Come on!— [*Leading her.*]
My little darling fell asleep! Come on— [*They go. Far
away beyond the orchard a shepherd is playing on a pipe.*
TROFIMOFF *walks across the stage and, seeing* VARYA *and*
ANYA, *stops.*] Shh— She is asleep—asleep— Let's go,
dear.

ANYA. [*Softly, half dreaming.*] I'm so tired— All the
bells!—Uncle—dear— And Mama and Uncle—Varya.

VARYA. Come on, my dear, come on. [*They go into* ANYA'S
room.]

TROFIMOFF. [*Tenderly.*] My little sun! My spring!

CURTAIN

ACT TWO

ACT TWO

A field. An old chapel, long abandoned, with crooked walls, near it a well, big stones that apparently were once tombstones, and an old bench. A road to the estate of GAYEFF *can be seen. On one side poplars rise, casting their shadows, the cherry orchard begins there. In the distance a row of telegraph poles; and far, far away, faintly traced on the horizon, is a large town, visible only in the clearest weather. The sun will soon be down.* CHARLOTTA, YASHA *and* DUNYASHA *are sitting on the bench;* EPIHODOFF *is standing near and playing the guitar; everyone sits lost in thought.* CHARLOTTA *wears an old peak cap [fourrage]; she has taken a rifle from off her shoulders and is adjusting the buckle on the strap.*

CHARLOTTA. [*Pensively.*] I have no proper passport, I don't know how old I am—it always seems to me I'm very young. When I was a little girl, my father and mother travelled from fair to fair and gave performances, very good ones. And I did *salto mortale* and different tricks. And when Papa and Mama died, a German lady took me to live with her and began teaching me. Good. I grew up. And became a governess. But where I came from and who I am I don't know— Who my parents were, perhaps they weren't even married—I don't know. [*Taking a cucumber out of her pocket and beginning to eat it.*] I don't know a thing. [*A pause.*] I'd like so much to talk but there's not anybody. I haven't anybody.

EPIHODOFF. [*Playing the guitar and singing.*] "What care I for the noisy world, what care I for friends and foes." —How pleasant it is to play the mandolin!

DUNYASHA. That's a guitar, not a mandolin. [*Looking into a little mirror and powdering her face.*]

EPIHODOFF. For a madman who is in love this is a mandolin— [*Singing.*] "If only my heart were warm with the fire of requited love."

[YASHA *sings with him.*]

CHARLOTTA. How dreadfully these people sing— Phooey! Like jackals.

DUNYASHA. [*To* YASHA.] All the same what happiness to have been abroad.

YASHA. Yes, of course. I cannot disagree with you.

[*Yawning and then lighting a cigar.*]

EPIHODOFF. That's easily understood. Abroad everything long since attained its complete development.

YASHA. That's obvious.

EPIHODOFF. I am a cultured man. I read all kinds of remarkable books, but the trouble is I cannot discover my own inclinations, whether to live or to shoot myself, but nevertheless, I always carry a revolver on me. Here it is —[*Showing a revolver.*]

CHARLOTTA. That's done. Now I am going. [*Slinging the rifle over her shoulder.*] You are a very clever man, Epihodoff, and a very terrible one; the women must love you madly. Brrrr-r-r-r! [*Going.*] These clever people are all so silly, I haven't anybody to talk with. I'm always alone, alone, I have nobody and— Who I am, why I am, is unknown— [*Goes out without hurrying.*]

EPIHODOFF. Strictly speaking, not touching on other subjects, I must state about myself, in passing, that fate treats me mercilessly, as a storm does a small ship. If, let us suppose, I am mistaken, then why, to mention one instance, do I wake up this morning, look and there on my chest is a spider of terrific size— There, like that. [*Showing the size with both hands.*] And also I take some kvass to drink and in it I find something in the highest degree indecent, such as a cockroach. [*A pause.*] Have you read Buckle? [*A pause.*] I desire to trouble you, Avdotya Feodorovna, with a couple of words.

DUNYASHA. Speak.

EPIHODOFF. I have a desire to speak with you alone— [*Sighing.*]

DUNYASHA. [*Embarrassed.*] Very well— But bring me my cape first—by the cupboard— It's rather damp here—

EPIHODOFF. Very well—I'll fetch it— Now I know what I should do with my revolver—[*Takes the guitar and goes out playing.*]

YASHA. Twenty-two misfortunes! Between us he's a stupid man, it must be said. [*Yawning.*]

DUNYASHA. God forbid he should shoot himself. [*A

pause.] I've grown so uneasy, I'm always fretting. I was only a girl when I was taken into the master's house, and now I've lost the habit of simple living—and here are my hands white, white as a lady's. I've become so delicate, fragile, lady-like, afraid of everything—Frightfully so. And, Yasha, if you deceive me, I don't know what will happen to my nerves.

YASHA. [*Kissing her.*] You little cucumber! Of course every girl must behave properly. What I dislike above everything is for a girl to conduct herself badly.

DUNYASHA. I have come to love you passionately, you are educated, you can discuss anything. [*A pause.*]

YASHA. [*Yawning.*] Yes, Sir—To my mind it is like this: If a girl loves someone, it means she is immoral. [*A pause.*] It is pleasant to smoke a cigar in the clear air— [*Listening.*] They are coming here— It is the ladies and gentlemen—

[DUNYASHA *impulsively embraces him.*]

YASHA. Go to the house, as though you had been to bathe in the river, go by this path, otherwise, they might meet you and suspect me of making a rendezvous with you. That I cannot tolerate.

DUNYASHA. [*With a little cough.*] Your cigar has given me the headache. [*Goes out.*]

[YASHA *remains, sitting near the chapel.* LYUBOFF ANDREY-EVNA, GAYEFF *and* LOPAHIN *enter.*]

LOPAHIN. We must decide definitely, time doesn't wait.

Why, the matter's quite simple. Are you willing to lease your land for summer cottages or are you not? Answer in one word, yes or no? Just one word!

LYUBOFF ANDREYEVNA. Who is it smokes those disgusting cigars out here—? [*Sitting down.*]

GAYEFF. The railroad running so near is a great convenience. [*Sitting down.*] We made a trip to town and lunched there— Yellow in the side pocket! Perhaps I should go in the house first and play one game—

LYUBOFF ANDREYEVNA. You'll have time.

LOPAHIN. Just one word! [*Imploringly.*] Do give me your answer!

GAYEFF. [*Yawning.*] What?

LYUBOFF ANDREYEVNA. [*Looking in her purse.*] Yesterday there was lots of money in it. Today there's very little. My poor Varya! For the sake of economy she feeds everybody milk soup, and in the kitchen the old people get nothing but beans, and here I spend money—senselessly— [*Dropping her purse and scattering gold coins.*] There they go scattering! [*She is vexed.*]

YASHA. Allow me, I'll pick them up in a second. [*Picking up the coins.*]

LYUBOFF ANDREYEVNA. If you will, Yasha. And why did I go in town for lunch—? Your restaurant with its music is trashy, the tablecloths smell of soap— Why drink so much, Lyonya? Why eat so much? Why talk so much? Today in the restaurant you were talking a lot again, and all of it beside the point. About the seventies, about the decadents. And to whom? Talking to waiters about the decadents!

LOPAHIN. Yes.

GAYEFF. [*Waving his hand.*] I am incorrigible, that's evident— [*To* YASHA *irritably.*] What is it?—You are forever swirling around in front of us?

YASHA. [*Laughing.*] I cannot hear your voice without laughing.

GAYEFF. [*To his sister.*] Either I or he—

LYUBOFF ANDREYEVNA. Go away, Yasha. Go on—

YASHA. [*Giving* LYUBOFF ANDREYEVNA *her purse.*] I am going right away. [*Barely suppressing his laughter.*] This minute. [*Goes out.*]

LOPAHIN. The rich Deriganoff intends to buy your estate. They say he is coming personally to the auction.

LYUBOFF ANDREYEVNA. And where did you hear that?

LOPAHIN. In town they are saying it.

GAYEFF. Our Yaroslavl aunt promised to send us something, but when and how much she will send, nobody knows—

LOPAHIN. How much will she send? A hundred thousand? Two hundred?

LYUBOFF ANDREYEVNA. Well,—maybe ten, fifteen thousand—we'd be thankful for that.

LOPAHIN. Excuse me, but such light-minded people as you are, such odd, unbusinesslike people, I never saw. You are told in plain Russian that your estate is being sold up and you just don't seem to take it in.

LYUBOFF ANDREYEVNA. But what are we to do? Tell us what?

LOPAHIN. I tell you every day. Every day I tell you the same thing. Both the cherry orchard and the land have got to be leased for summer cottages, it has to be done right now, quick— The auction is right under your noses. Do understand! Once you finally decide that there are to be summer cottages, you will get all the money you want, and then you'll be saved.

LYUBOFF ANDREYEVNA. Summer cottages and summer residents—it is so trivial, excuse me.

GAYEFF. I absolutely agree with you.

LOPAHIN. I'll either burst out crying, or scream, or faint. I can't bear it! You are torturing me! [*To* GAYEFF.] You're a perfect old woman!

GAYEFF. What?

LOPAHIN. A perfect old woman! [*About to go.*]

LYUBOFF ANDREYEVNA. [*Alarmed.*] No, don't go, stay, my lamb, I beg you. Perhaps we will think of something!

LOPAHIN. What is there to think about?

LYUBOFF ANDREYEVNA. Don't go, I beg you. With you here it is more cheerful anyhow— [*A pause.*] I keep waiting for something, as if the house were about to tumble down on our heads.

GAYEFF. [*Deep in thought.*] Double into the corner pocket. —Bank into the side pocket—

LYUBOFF ANDREYEVNA. We have sinned so much—

LOPAHIN. What sins have you—?

GAYEFF. [*Puts a hard candy into his mouth.*] They say I've eaten my fortune up in hard candies— [*Laughing.*]

LYUBOFF ANDREYEVNA. Oh, my sins—I've always thrown money around like mad, recklessly, and I married a man who accumulated nothing but debts. My husband died from champagne—he drank fearfully—and to my misfortune I fell in love with another man. I lived with him, and just at that time—it was my first punishment—a blow over the head: right here in the river my boy was drowned and I went abroad—went away for good, never to return, never to see this river again—I shut my eyes, ran away, beside myself, and he after me—mercilessly, brutally. I bought a villa near Mentone, because he fell ill there, and for three years I knew no rest day or night, the sick man exhausted me, my soul dried up. And last year when the villa was sold for debts, I went to Paris and there he robbed me of everything, threw me over, took up with another woman; I tried to poison myself—so stupid, so shameful— And suddenly I was seized with longing for Russia, for my own country, for my little girl— [*Wiping away her tears.*] Lord, Lord, have mercy, forgive me my sins! Don't punish me any more! [*Getting a telegram out of her pocket.*] I got this today from

Paris, he asks forgiveness, begs me to return— [*Tears up the telegram.*] That sounds like music somewhere.

[*Listening.*]

GAYEFF. It is our famous Jewish orchestra. You remember, four violins, a flute and double bass.

LYUBOFF ANDREYEVNA. Does it still exist? We ought to get hold of it sometime and give a party.

LOPAHIN. [*Listening.*] Can't hear it— [*Singing softly.*] "And for money the Germans will frenchify a Russian." [*Laughing.*] What a play I saw yesterday at the theatre, very funny!

LYUBOFF ANDREYEVNA. And most likely there was nothing funny about it. You shouldn't look at plays, but look oftener at yourselves. How gray all your lives are, what a lot of idle things you say!

LOPAHIN. That's true. It must be said frankly this life of ours is idiotic— [*A pause.*] My father was a peasant, an idiot, he understood nothing, he taught me nothing, he just beat me in his drunken fits and always with a stick. At bottom I am just as big a dolt and idiot as he was. I wasn't taught anything, my handwriting is vile, I write like a pig—I am ashamed for people to see it.

LYUBOFF ANDREYEVNA. You ought to get married, my friend.

LOPAHIN. Yes—That's true.

LYUBOFF ANDREYEVNA. To our Varya, perhaps. She is a good girl.

LOPAHIN. Yes.

LYUBOFF ANDREYEVNA. She comes from simple people, and she works all day long, but the main thing is she loves you. And you, too, have liked her a long time.

LOPAHIN. Why not? I am not against it— She's a good girl. [*A pause.*]

GAYEFF. They are offering me a position in a bank. Six thousand a year— Have you heard that?

LYUBOFF ANDREYEVNA. Not you! You stay where you are—

FIERS. [FIERS *enters, bringing an overcoat. To* GAYEFF.] Pray, Sir, put this on, it's damp.

GAYEFF. [*Putting on the overcoat.*] You're a pest, old man.

FIERS. That's all right— This morning you went off without letting me know. [*Looking him over.*]

LYUBOFF ANDREYEVNA. How old you've grown, Fiers!

FIERS. At your service.

LOPAHIN. She says you've grown very old!

FIERS. I've lived a long time. They were planning to marry me off before your papa was born. [*Laughing.*] And at the time the serfs were freed I was already the head footman. I didn't want to be freed then, I stayed with the masters—[*A pause.*] And I remember, everybody was happy, but what they were happy about they didn't know themselves.

LOPAHIN. In the old days it was fine. At least they flogged.

FIERS. [*Not hearing.*] But, of course. The peasants stuck to the masters, the masters stuck to the peasants, and now everything is all smashed up, you can't tell about anything.

GAYEFF. Keep still, Fiers. Tomorrow I must go to town. They have promised to introduce me to a certain general who might make us a loan.

LOPAHIN. Nothing will come of it. And you can rest assured you won't pay the interest.

LYUBOFF ANDREYEVNA. He's just raving on. There aren't any such generals.

[TROFIMOFF, ANYA *and* VARYA *enter.*]

GAYEFF. Here they come.

ANYA. There is Mama sitting there.

LYUBOFF ANDREYEVNA. [*Tenderly.*] Come, come—My darlings—[*Embracing* ANYA *and* VARYA.] If you only knew how I love you both! Come sit by me, there—like that.

[EVERYBODY *sits down.*]

LOPAHIN. Our perennial student is always strolling with the young ladies.

TROFIMOFF. It's none of your business.

LOPAHIN. He will soon be fifty and he's still a student.

TROFIMOFF. Stop your stupid jokes.

LOPAHIN. But why are you so peevish, you queer duck?

TROFIMOFF. Don't you pester me.

LOPAHIN. [*Laughing.*] Permit me to ask you, what do you make of me?

TROFIMOFF. Yermolay Alexeyevitch, I make this of you: you are a rich man, you'll soon be a millionaire. Just as it is in the metabolism of nature, a wild beast is needed to eat up everything that comes his way; so you, too, are needed.

[EVERYONE *laughs.*]

VARYA. Petya, you'd better tell us about the planets.

LYUBOFF ANDREYEVNA. No, let's go on with yesterday's conversation.

TROFIMOFF. What was it about?

GAYEFF. About the proud man.

TROFIMOFF. We talked a long time yesterday, but didn't get anywhere. In a proud man, in your sense of the word there is something mystical. Maybe you are right, from your standpoint, but if we are to discuss it in simple terms, without whimsy, then what pride can there be, is there any sense in it, if man physiologically is poorly constructed, if in the great majority he is crude, unintelligent, profoundly miserable. One must stop admiring one's self. One must only work.

GAYEFF. All the same, you will die.

TROFIMOFF. Who knows? And what does it mean—you will die? Man may have a hundred senses, and when he dies only the five that are known to us may perish, and the remaining ninety-five go on living.

LYUBOFF ANDREYEVNA. How clever you are, Petya!

LOPAHIN. [*Ironically.*] Terribly!

TROFIMOFF. Humanity goes forward, perfecting its powers. Everything that's unattainable now will some day become familiar, understandable; it is only that one must work and must help with all one's might those who seek the truth. With us in Russia so far only a very few work. The great majority of the intelligentsia that I know are looking for nothing, doing nothing, and as yet have no capacity for work. They call themselves intelligentsia, are free and easy with the servants, treat the peasants like animals, educate themselves poorly, read nothing seriously, do absolutely nothing; about science they just talk and about art they understand very little. Every one of them is serious, all have stern faces; they all talk of nothing but important things, philosophize, and all the time everybody can see that the workmen eat abominably, sleep without any pillows, thirty or forty to a room, and everywhere there are bedbugs, stench, dampness, moral uncleanness— And apparently with us, all the fine talk is only to divert the attention of ourselves and of others. Show me where we have the day-nurseries they are always talking so much about, where are the reading rooms? They only write of these in novels, for the truth is there are not any at all. There is only filth, vulgarity, orientalism— I am afraid of very serious faces and dislike them. I'm afraid of serious conversations. Rather than that let's just keep still.

LOPAHIN. You know I get up before five o'clock in the morning and work from morning till night. Well, I always have money, my own and other people's, on hand, and I see what the people around me are. One has only to start doing something to find out how few honest and decent people there are. At times when I can't go to sleep, I think: Lord, thou gavest us immense forests, unbounded fields and the widest horizons, and living in the midst of them we should indeed be giants—

LYUBOFF ANDREYEVNA. You feel the need for giants.— They are good only in fairy tales, anywhere else they only frighten us.

[*At the back of the stage* EPIHODOFF *passes by, playing the guitar.*]

LYUBOFF ANDREYEVNA. [*Lost in thought.*] Epihodoff is coming—

ANYA. [*Lost in thought.*] Epihodoff is coming

GAYEFF. The sun has set, ladies and gentlemen.

TROFIMOFF. Yes.

GAYEFF. [*Not loud and as if he were declaiming.*] Oh, Nature, wonderful, you gleam with eternal radiance, beautiful and indifferent, you, whom we call Mother, combine in yourself both life and death, you give life and you take it away.

VARYA. [*Beseechingly.*] Uncle!

ANYA. Uncle, you're doing it again!

TROFIMOFF. You'd better bank the yellow into the side pocket.

GAYEFF. I'll be quiet, quiet.

[ALL *sit absorbed in their thoughts. There is only the silence.* FIERS *is heard muttering to himself softly. Suddenly a distant sound is heard, as if from the sky, like the sound of a snapped string, dying away, mournful.*]

LYUBOFF ANDREYEVNA. What's that?

LOPAHIN. I don't know. Somewhere far off in a mine shaft a bucket fell. But somewhere very far off.

GAYEFF. And it may be some bird—like a heron

TROFIMOFF. Or an owl—

LYUBOFF ANDREYEVNA. [*Shivering.*] It's unpleasant, somehow. [*A pause.*]

FIERS. Before the disaster it was like that. The owl hooted and the samovar hummed without stopping, both.

GAYEFF. Before what disaster?

FIERS. Before the emancipation.

[*A pause.*]

LYUBOFF ANDREYEVNA. You know, my friends, let's go. Twilight is falling. [*To* ANYA.] You have tears in your eyes— What is it, my dear little girl? [*Embracing her.*]

ANYA. It's just that, Mama. It's nothing.

TROFIMOFF. Somebody is coming.

[*A* STRANGER *appears in a shabby white cap, and an overcoat; he is a little drunk.*]

THE STRANGER. Allow me to ask you, can I go straight through here to the station?

GAYEFF. You can. Go by that road.

THE STRANGER. I am heartily grateful to you. [*Coughing.*] The weather is splendid— [*Declaiming.*] Brother of mine, suffering brother— Go out to the Volga, whose moans— [*To* VARYA.] Mademoiselle, grant a hungry Russian man some thirty kopecks—

[VARYA *is frightened and gives a shriek.*]

LOPAHIN. [*Angrily.*] There's a limit to everything.

LYUBOFF ANDREYEVNA. [*Flustered.*] Take this— Here's this for you— [*Searching in her purse.*] No silver— It's all the same, here's a gold piece for you—

THE STRANGER. I am heartily grateful to you. [*Goes out. Laughter.*]

VARYA. [*Frightened.*] I'm going—I'm going— Oh, Mama, you poor little Mama! There's nothing in the house for people to eat, and you gave him a gold piece.

LYUBOFF ANDREYEVNA. What is to be done with me, so silly? I shall give you all I have in the house. Yermolay Alexeyevitch, you will lend me some this once more!—

LOPAHIN. Agreed.

LYUBOFF ANDREYEVNA. Let's go, ladies and gentlemen, it's time. And here, Varya, we have definitely made a match for you, I congratulate you.

VARYA. [*Through her tears.*] Mama, that's not something to joke about.

LOPAHIN. Achmelia, get thee to a nunnery.

GAYEFF. And my hands are trembling; it is a long time since I have played billiards.

LOPAHIN. Achmelia, O nymph, in thine orisons be all my sins remember'd—

LYUBOFF ANDREYEVNA. Let's go, my dear friends, it will soon be supper time.

VARYA. He frightened me. My heart is thumping so.

LOPAHIN. I remind you, ladies and gentlemen: August 22nd the cherry orchard will be auctioned off. Think about that !—Think !—

[ALL *go out except* TROFIMOFF *and* ANYA.]

ANYA. [*Laughing.*] My thanks to the stranger, he frightened Varya, now we are alone.

TROFIMOFF. Varya is afraid we might begin to love each other and all day long she won't leave us to ourselves. With her narrow mind she cannot understand that we are above love. To sidestep the petty and illusory, which prevent our being free and happy, that is the aim and meaning of our life. Forward! We march on irresistibly toward the bright star that burns there in the distance. Forward! Do not fall behind, friends!

ANYA. [*Extending her arms upward.*] How well you talk! [*A pause.*] It's wonderful here today!

TROFIMOFF. Yes, the weather is marvelous.

ANYA. What have you done to me, Petya, why don't I

love the cherry orchard any longer the way I used to? I loved it so tenderly, it seemed to me there was not a better place on earth than our orchard.

TROFIMOFF. All Russia is our orchard. The earth is immense and beautiful, and on it are many wonderful places. [*A pause.*] Just think, Anya: your grandfather, great-grandfather and all your ancestors were slave owners, in possession of living souls, and can you doubt that from every cherry in the orchard, from every leaf, from every trunk, human beings are looking at you, can it be that you don't hear their voices? To possess living souls, well, that depraved all of you who lived before and who are living now, so that your mother and you, and your uncle no longer notice that you live by debt, at somebody else's expense, at the expense of those very people whom you wouldn't let past your front door— We are at least two hundred years behind the times, we have as yet absolutely nothing, we have no definite attitude toward the past, we only philosophize, complain of our sadness or drink vodka. Why, it is quite clear that to begin to live in the present we must first atone for our past, must be done with it; and we can atone for it only through suffering, only through uncommon, incessant labor. Understand that, Anya.

ANYA. The house we live in ceased to be ours long ago, and I'll go away, I give you my word.

TROFIMOFF. If you have the household keys, throw them in the well and go away. Be free as the wind.

ANYA. [*Transported.*] How well you said that!

TROFIMOFF. Believe me, Anya, believe me! I am not thirty yet, I am young, I am still a student, but I have already borne so much! Every winter I am hungry, sick, anxious, poor as a beggar, and—where has destiny not chased me, where haven't I been! And yet, my soul has always, every minute, day and night, been full of inexplicable premonitions. I have a premonition of happiness, Anya, I see it already—

ANYA. [*Pensively.*] The moon is rising.

[EPIHODOFF *is heard playing on the guitar, always the same sad song. The moon rises. Somewhere near the poplars* VARYA *is looking for* ANYA *and calling: "Anya! Where are you?"*]

TROFIMOFF. Yes, the moon is rising. [*A pause.*] Here is happiness, here it comes, comes always nearer and nearer, I hear its footsteps now. And if we shall not see it, shall not come to know it, what does that matter? Others will see it!

VARYA. [*Off.*] Anya! Where are you?

TROFIMOFF. Again, that Varya! [*Angrily.*] It's scandalous!

ANYA. Well, let's go to the river. It's lovely there.

TROFIMOFF. Let's go. [*They go out.*]

VARYA. [*Off.*] Anya! Anya!

CURTAIN

ACT THREE

ACT THREE

*The drawing room, separated by an arch from the ball-
room. A chandelier is lighted. A Jewish orchestra is playing—the same that was mentioned in Act II. Evening.
In the ballroom they are dancing* grand rond. *The voice
of* SEMYONOFF-PISHTCHIK: *"Promenade à une paire!"
They enter the drawing room; in the first couple are*
PISHTCHIK *and* CHARLOTTA IVANOVNA; *in the second,*
TROFIMOFF *and* LYUBOFF ANDREYEVNA; *in the third,* ANYA
with the POST-OFFICE CLERK; *in the fourth,* VARYA *with
the* STATION MASTER, *et cetera—*VARYA *is crying softly
and wipes away her tears while she is dancing.* DUNYASHA
is in the last couple through the drawing room, PISHTCHIK
*shouts: "Grand rond, balancez!" and "Les Cavaliers à
genoux et remerciez vos dames!"*
[FIERS *in a frock coat goes by with seltzer water on a
tray.* PISHTCHIK *and* TROFIMOFF *come into the drawing
room.*]

PISHTCHIK. I am full-blooded, I have had two strokes
already, and dancing is hard for me, but as they say, if
you are in a pack of dogs, you may bark and bark, but
you must still wag your tail. At that, I have the health of
a horse. My dear father—he was a great joker—may he
dwell in Heaven—used to talk as if our ancient line, the
Semyonoff-Pishtchiks, were descended from the very

53

horse that Caligula made a Senator— [*Sitting down.*] But here's my trouble: I haven't any money. A hungry dog believes in nothing but meat— [*Snoring but waking at once.*] And the same way with me—I can't talk about anything but money.

TROFIMOFF. Well, to tell you the truth, there is something of a horse about your figure.

PISHTCHIK. Well,—a horse is a fine animal— You can sell a horse—

[*The sound of playing billiards comes from the next room. VARYA appears under the arch to the ballroom.*]

TROFIMOFF. [*Teasing.*] Madam Lopahin! Madam Lopahin!

VARYA. [*Angrily.*] A mangy-looking gentleman!

TROFIMOFF. Yes, I am a mangy-looking gentleman, and proud of it!

VARYA. [*In bitter thought.*] Here we have gone and hired musicians and what are we going to pay them with?

[*Goes out.*]

TROFIMOFF. [*To PISHTCHIK.*] If the energy you have wasted in the course of your life trying to find money to pay the interest had gone into something else, you could very likely have turned the world upside down before you were done with it.

PISHTCHIK. Nietzsche—the philosopher—the greatest— the most celebrated—a man of tremendous mind—says in his works that one may make counterfeit money.

TROFIMOFF. And have you read Nietzsche?

PISHTCHIK. Well—Dashenka told me. And I'm in such a state now that I could make counterfeit money myself.— Day after tomorrow three hundred and ten roubles must be paid—one hundred and thirty I've on hand— [*Feeling in his pockets, alarmed.*] The money is gone! I have lost the money! [*Tearfully.*] Where is the money? [*Joyfully.*] Here it is, inside the lining—I was in quite a sweat—

[LYUBOFF ANDREYEVNA *and* CHARLOTTA IVANOVNA *come in.*]

LYUBOFF ANDREYEVNA. [*Humming lazginka, a Georgian dance.*] Why does Leonid take so long? What's he doing in town? [*To* DUNYASHA.] Dunyasha, offer the musicians some tea—

TROFIMOFF. In all probability the auction did not take place.

LYUBOFF ANDREYEVNA. And the musicians came at an unfortunate moment and we planned the ball at an unfortunate moment— Well, it doesn't matter. [*Sitting down and singing softly.*]

CHARLOTTA. [*Gives* PISHTCHIK *a deck of cards.*] Here is a deck of cards for you, think of some one card.

PISHTCHIK. I have thought of one.

CHARLOTTA. Now, shuffle the deck. Very good. Hand it here; oh, my dear Monsieur Pishtchik. Ein, zwei, drei! Now look for it, it's in your coat pocket—

PISHTCHIK. [*Getting a card out of his coat pocket.*] The

eight of spades, that's absolutely right! [*Amazed.*] Fancy that!

CHARLOTTA. [*Holding a deck of cards in her palm; to* TROFIMOFF.] Tell me quick now, which card is on top?

TROFIMOFF. What is it? Well—the Queen of Spades.

CHARLOTTA. Right! [*To* PISHTCHIK.] Well? Which card's on top?

PISHTCHIK. The Ace of Hearts.

CHARLOTTA. Right!—[*Strikes the deck against her palm, the deck of cards disappears.*] And what beautiful weather we are having today!

[*A mysterious* FEMININE VOICE *answers her, as if from under the floor:* "Oh, yes. The weather is splendid, Madame." "You are so nice, you're my ideal—"* THE VOICE. "Madam, you too please me greatly."]

THE STATION MASTER. [*Applauding.*] Madam Ventriloquist, bravo!

PISHTCHIK. [*Amazed.*] Fancy that! Most charming Charlotta Ivanovna—I am simply in love with you.

CHARLOTTA. In love? [*Shrugging her shoulders.*] Is it possible that you can love? *Guter menschaber schlachter musikant.*

TROFIMOFF. [*Slapping* PISHTCHIK *on the shoulder.*] You horse, you—

CHARLOTTA. I beg your attention, one more trick. [*Taking a lap-robe from the chair.*] Here is a very fine lap-robe—

I want to sell it— [*Shaking it out.*] Wouldn't somebody like to buy it?

PISHTCHIK. [*Amazed.*] Fancy that!

CHARLOTTA. Ein, zwei, drei!

[*She quickly raises the lowered robe, behind it stands* ANYA, *who curtseys, runs to her mother, embraces her and runs back into the ballroom amid the general delight.*]

LYUBOFF ANDREYEVNA. [*Applauding.*] Bravo, bravo—!

CHARLOTTA. Now again! Ein, zwei, drei!

[*Lifting the robe: behind it stands* VARYA, *she bows.*]

PISHTCHIK. [*Amazed.*] Fancy that!

CHARLOTTA. That's all. [*Throwing the robe at* PISHTCHIK, *curtseying and running into the ballroom.*]

PISHTCHIK. [*Hurrying after her.*] You little rascal— What a girl? What a girl? [*Goes out.*]

LYUBOFF ANDREYEVNA. And Leonid is not here yet. What he's doing in town so long, I don't understand! Everything is finished there, either the estate is sold by now, or the auction didn't take place. Why keep it from us so long?

VARYA. [*Trying to comfort her.*] Uncle has bought it, I am sure of that.

TROFIMOFF. [*Mockingly.*] Yes.

VARYA. Grandmother sent him power of attorney to buy it in her name and transfer the debt. She did this for Anya. And I feel certain, God willing, that Uncle will buy it.

LYUBOFF ANDREYEVNA. Our Yaroslavl grandmother has sent fifteen thousand to buy the estate in her name— She doesn't trust us, but that wouldn't be enough to pay the interest even— [*Covering her face with her hands.*] Today my fate will be decided, my fate—

TROFIMOFF [*Teasing* VARYA.] Madam Lopahin!

VARYA. [*Angrily.*] Perennial student! You have already been expelled from the University twice.

LYUBOFF ANDREYEVNA. But why are you angry, Varya? He teases you about Lopahin, what of it? Marry Lopahin if you want to, he is a good man, interesting. If you don't want to, don't marry him; darling, nobody is making you do it.

VARYA. I look at this matter seriously, Mama, one must speak straight out. He's a good man, I like him.

LYUBOFF ANDREYEVNA. Then marry him. What there is to wait for I don't understand!

VARYA. But I can't propose to him myself, Mama. It's two years now; everyone has been talking to me about him, everyone talks, and he either remains silent or jokes. I understand. He's getting rich, he's busy with his own affairs, and has no time for me. If there were money, ever so little, even a hundred roubles, I would drop everything, and go far away. I'd go to a nunnery.

TROFIMOFF. How saintly!

VARYA. [*To* TROFIMOFF.] A student should be intelligent! [*In a low voice, tearfully.*] How homely you have grown,

Petya, how old you've got. [*To* LYUBOFF ANDREYEVNA, *no longer crying.*] It is just that I can't live without working, Mama. I must be doing something every minute.

YASHA. [YASHA *enters. Barely restraining his laughter.*] Epihodoff has broken a billiard cue!— [*Goes out.*]

VARYA. But why is Epihodoff here? Who allowed him to play billiards? I don't understand these people— [*Goes out.*]

LYUBOFF ANDREYEVNA. Don't tease her, Petya; you can see she has troubles enough without that.

TROFIMOFF. She is just too zealous. Sticking her nose into things that are none of her business. All summer she gave us no peace, neither me nor Anya; she was afraid a romance would spring up between us. What business is that of hers? And besides I haven't shown any signs of it. I am so remote from triviality. We are above love!

LYUBOFF ANDREYEVNA. Well, then, I must be beneath love. [*Very anxiously.*] Why isn't Leonid here? Just to tell us whether the estate is sold or not? Calamity seems to me so incredible that I don't know what to think, I'm lost—I could scream this minute—I could do something insane. Save me, Petya. Say something, do say—

TROFIMOFF. Whether the estate is sold today or is not sold —is it not the same? There is no turning back, the path is all grown over. Calm yourself, my dear, all that was over long ago. One mustn't deceive oneself, one must for once at least in one's life look truth straight in the eye.

LYUBOFF ANDREYEVNA. What truth? You see where the

truth is and where the untruth is, but as for me, it's as if I had lost my sight, I see nothing. You boldly decide all important questions, but tell me, my dear boy, isn't that because you are young and haven't had time yet to suffer through any one of your problems? You look boldly ahead, and isn't that because you don't see and don't expect anything terrible, since life is still hidden from your young eyes? You are braver, more honest, more profound than we are, but stop and think, be magnanimous, have a little mercy on me, just a little. Why, I was born here. My father and mother lived here and my grandfather. I love this house, I can't imagine my life without the cherry orchard and if it is very necessary to sell it, then sell me along with the orchard— [*Embracing* TRO- FIMOFF *and kissing him on the forehead.*] Why, my son was drowned here—[*Crying.*] Have mercy on me, good, kind man.

TROFIMOFF. You know I sympathize with you from the bottom of my heart.

LYUBOFF ANDREYEVNA. But that should be said differently, differently—[*Taking out her handkerchief, a telegram falls on the floor.*] My heart is heavy today, you can't imagine how heavy. It is too noisy for me here, my soul trembles at every sound, I tremble all over and yet I can't go off to myself, when I am alone the silence frightens me. Don't blame me, Petya—I love you as one of my own. I should gladly have given you Anya's hand, I assure you, only, my dear, you must study and finish your course. You do nothing, Fate simply flings you about from place to place, and that's so strange— Isn't that so?

Yes? And you must do something about your beard, to make it grow somehow— [*Laughing.*] You look funny! TROFIMOFF. [*Picking up the telegram.*] I do not desire to be beautiful.

LYUBOFF ANDREYEVNA. This telegram is from Paris. I get one every day. Yesterday and today too. That wild man has fallen ill again, something is wrong again with him.— He asks forgiveness, begs me to come, and really I ought to make a trip to Paris and stay awhile near him. Your face looks stern, Petya, but what is there to do, my dear, what am I to do, he is ill, he is alone, unhappy and who will look after him there, who will keep him from doing the wrong thing, who will give him his medicine on time? And what is there to hide or keep still about? I love him, that's plain. I love him, love him— It's a stone about my neck, I'm sinking to the bottom with it, but I love that stone and live without it I cannot. [*Pressing* TROFIMOFF'S *hand.*] Don't think harshly of me, Petya, don't say anything to me, don't—

TROFIMOFF. [*Tearfully.*] Forgive my frankness, for God's sake! Why, he picked your bones.

LYUBOFF ANDREYEVNA. No, no, no, you must not talk like that. [*Stopping her ears.*]

TROFIMOFF. But he is a scoundrel, only you, you are the only one that doesn't know it. He is a petty scoundrel, a nonentity—

LYUBOFF ANDREYEVNA. [*Angry but controlling herself.*] You are twenty-six years old or twenty-seven, but you are still a schoolboy in the second grade!

TROFIMOFF. Very well!

LYUBOFF ANDREYEVNA. You should be a man—at your age you should understand people who love. And you yourself should love someone—you should fall in love! [*Angrily.*] Yes, yes! And there is no purity in you; you are simply smug, a ridiculous crank, a freak—

TROFIMOFF. [*Horrified.*] What is she saying!

LYUBOFF ANDREYEVNA. "I am above love!" You are not above love, Petya, you are, as our Fiers would say, just a good-for-nothing. Imagine, at your age, not having a mistress—!

TROFIMOFF. [*Horrified.*] This is terrible! What is she saying! [*Goes quickly into the ballroom, clutching his head.*] This is horrible—I can't bear it, I am going— [*Goes out but immediately returns.*] All is over between us. [*Goes out into the hall.*]

LYUBOFF ANDREYEVNA. [*Shouting after him.*] Petya, wait! You funny creature, I was joking! Petya! [*In the hall you hear someone running up the stairs and suddenly falling back down with a crash. You hear* ANYA *and* VARYA *scream but immediately you hear laughter.*] What's that? ANYA. [ANYA *runs in. Laughing.*] Petya fell down the stairs! [*Runs out.*]

LYUBOFF ANDREYEVNA. What a funny boy that Petya is—! [*The* STATION-MASTER *stops in the Center of the ballroom and begins to recite "The Sinner" by A. Tolstoy. They listen to him but he has recited only a few lines when the strains of a waltz are heard from the hall and the recita-*

tion is broken off. They ALL *dance.* TROFIMOFF, ANYA, VARYA *and* LYUBOFF ANDREYEVNA *come in from the hall.*] But, Petya—but, dear soul—I beg your forgiveness— Let's go dance.

[*She dances with* TROFIMOFF, ANYA *and* VARYA *dance.* FIERS *enters, leaving his stick by the side door.* YASHA *also comes into the drawing-room and watches the dancers.*] YASHA. What is it, Grandpa?

FIERS. I don't feel very well. In the old days there were generals, barons, admirals dancing at our parties, and now we send for the post-office clerk and the station master, and even they are none too anxious to come. Somehow I've grown feeble. The old master, the grandfather, treated everybody with sealing-wax for all sicknesses. I take sealing-wax every day, have done so for twenty-odd years or more; it may be due to that that I'm alive.

YASHA. You are tiresome, Grandpa. [*Yawning.*] Why don't you go off and die?

FIERS. Aw, you—good-for-nothing!— [*Muttering.*]

[TROFIMOFF *and* LYUBOFF ANDREYEVNA *dance in the ball-room and then in the drawing-room.*]

LYUBOFF ANDREYEVNA. *Merci.* I'll sit down awhile— [*Sitting down.*] I'm tired.

ANYA. [ANYA *enters. Agitated.*] And just now in the kitchen some man was saying that the cherry orchard had been sold today.

LYUBOFF ANDREYEVNA. Sold to whom?

ANYA. He didn't say who to. He's gone.

[*Dancing with* TROFIMOFF, *they pass into the ballroom.*]

YASHA. It was some old man babbling there. A stranger.

FIERS. And Leonid Andreyevitch is still not here, he has not arrived. The overcoat he has on is light, mid-season—let's hope he won't catch cold. Ach, these young things!

LYUBOFF ANDREYEVNA. I shall die this minute. Go, Yasha, find out who it was sold to.

YASHA. But he's been gone a long time, the old fellow.

[*Laughing.*]

LYUBOFF ANDREYEVNA. [*With some annoyance.*] Well, what are you laughing at? What are you so amused at?

YASHA. Epihodoff is just too funny. An empty-headed man. Twenty-two misfortunes.

LYUBOFF ANDREYEVNA. Fiers, if the estate is sold, where will you go?

FIERS. Wherever you say, there I'll go.

LYUBOFF ANDREYEVNA. Why do you look like that? Aren't you well? You know you ought to go to bed—

FIERS. Yes—[*With a sneer.*] I go to bed and without me who's going to serve, who'll take care of things? I'm the only one in the whole house.

YASHA. [*To* LYUBOFF ANDREYEVNA.] Lyuboff Andreyevna, let me ask a favor of you, do be so kind! If you ever go back to Paris, take me with you, please do! It's impossible for me to stay here. [*Looking around him, and speaking in a low voice.*] Why talk about it? You can see for yourself it's an uncivilized country, an immoral people and not only that, there's the boredom of it. The food they give us in that kitchen is abominable and there's that Fiers, too, walking about and muttering all kinds of words that are out of place. Take me with you, be so kind!

PISHTCHIK. [PISHTCHIK *enters.*] Allow me to ask you— for a little waltz, most beautiful lady— [LYUBOFF ANDRE-YEVNA *goes with him.*] Charming lady, I must borrow a hundred and eighty roubles from you—will borrow— [*Dancing.*] a hundred and eighty roubles— [*They pass into the ballroom.*]

YASHA. [*Singing low.*] "Wilt thou know the unrest in my soul!"

[*In the ballroom a figure in a gray top hat and checked trousers waves both hands and jumps about; there are shouts of "Bravo, Charlotta Ivanovna!"*]

DUNYASHA. [*Stopping to powder her face.*] The young lady orders me to dance—there are a lot of gentlemen and very few ladies—but dancing makes my head swim and my heart thump. Fiers Nikolayevitch, the post-office clerk said something to me just now that took my breath away.

[*The music plays more softly.*]

FIERS. What did he say to you?

DUNYASHA. You are like a flower, he says.

YASHA. [*Yawning.*] What ignorance—! [*Goes out.*]

DUNYASHA. Like a flower—I am such a sensitive girl, I love tender words awfully.

FIERS. You'll be getting your head turned.

[EPIHODOFF *enters.*]

EPIHODOFF. Avdotya Feodorovna, you don't want to see me— It's as if I were some sort of insect. [*Sighing.*] Ach, life!

DUNYASHA. What do you want?

EPIHODOFF. Undoubtedly you may be right. [*Sighing.*] But of course, if one considers it from a given point of view, then you, I will allow myself so to express it, forgive my frankness, absolutely led me into a state of mind. I know my fate, every day some misfortune happens to me, but I have long since become accustomed to that, and so I look on my misfortunes with a smile. You gave me your word and, although I—

DUNYASHA. I beg you, we'll talk later on, but leave me now in peace. I'm in a dream now. [*Playing with her fan.*]

EPIDOHOFF. I have a something wrong happens every day. —I will allow myself so to express it—I just smile, I even laugh.

VARYA. [VARYA *enters from the ballroom.*] You are not gone yet, Semyon? What a really disrespectful man you are! [*To* DUNYASHA.] Get out of here, Dunyasha. [*To* EPIHODOFF.] You either play billiards and break a cue or you walk about the drawing-room like a guest.

EPIHODOFF. Allow me to tell you, you cannot make any de- mands on me.

VARYA. I'm not making any demands on you, I'm talking to you. All you know is to walk from place to place but not do any work. We keep a clerk, but what for, nobody knows.

EPIHODOFF. [*Offended.*] Whether I work, whether I walk, whether I eat, or whether I play billiards are matters to be discussed only by people of understanding and my seniors.

VARYA. You dare to say that to me! [*Flying into a temper.*] You dare? So I don't understand anything? Get out of here! This minute!

EPIHODOFF. [*Alarmed.*] I beg you to express yourself in a delicate manner.

VARYA. [*Beside herself.*] This very minute, get out of here! Get out! [*He goes to the door, she follows him.*] Twenty-two misfortunes! Don't you dare breathe in here! Don't let me set eyes on you! [EPIHODOFF *has gone out, but his voice comes from outside the door: "I shall complain about you."*] Ah, you are coming back? [*Grabbing the stick that* FIERS *put by the door.*] Come on, come— come on, I'll show you.—Ah, you are coming? You are coming? Take that then—!

[*She swings the stick, at the very moment when* LOPAHIN *is coming in.*]

LOPAHIN. Most humbly, I thank you.

VARYA. [*Angrily and ironically.*] I beg your pardon!

LOPAHIN. It's nothing at all. I humbly thank you for the pleasant treat.

VARYA. It isn't worth your thanks. [*Moving away, then looking back and asking gently.*] I haven't hurt you?

LOPAHIN. No, it's nothing. There's a great bump coming though.

[VOICES *in the ballroom: "Lopahin has come back."* *"Yermolay Alexeyevitch!"*]

PISHTCHIK. [*Enters.*] See what we see, hear what we hear—! [*He and* LOPAHIN *kiss one another.*] You smell slightly of cognac, my dear, my good old chap. And we are amusing ourselves here too.

LYUBOFF ANDREYEVNA. [LYUBOFF ANDREYEVNA *enters.*] Is that you, Yermolay Alexeyevitch? Why were you so long? Where is Leonid?

LOPAHIN. Leonid Andreyevitch got back when I did, he's coming.

LYUBOFF ANDREYEVNA. [*Agitated.*] Well, what? Was there an auction? Do speak!

LOPAHIN. [*Embarrassed, afraid of showing the joy he feels.*] The auction was over by four o'clock— We were late for the train, had to wait till half-past nine. [*Sighing heavily.*] Ugh, my head's swimming a bit!

[GAYEFF *enters; with his right hand he carries his purchases, with his left he wipes away his tears.*]

LYUBOFF ANDREYEVNA. Lyona, what? Lyona, eh? *Impatiently, with tears in her eyes.*] Quick, for God's sake—
GAYEFF. [*Not answering her, merely waving his hand; to* FIERS, *crying.*] Here, take it— There are anchovies, some Kertch herrings— I haven't eaten anything all day— What I have suffered! [*The door into the billiard room is open; you hear the balls clicking and* YASHA'S *voice: "Seven*

and eighteen!" GAYEFF'S *expression changes, he is no longer crying.*] I'm terribly tired. You help me change, Fiers. [*Goes to his room through the ballroom,* FIERS *behind him.*]

PISHTCHIK. What happened at the auction? Go on, tell us!

LYUBOFF ANDREYEVNA. Is the cherry orchard sold?

LOPAHIN. It's sold.

LYUBOFF ANDREYEVNA. Who bought it?

LOPAHIN. I bought it. [*A pause.* LYUBOFF ANDREYEVNA *is overcome. She would have fallen had she not been standing near the chair and table.* VARYA *takes the keys from her belt, throws them on the floor in the middle of the drawing-room and goes out.*] I bought it. Kindly wait a moment, ladies and gentlemen, everything is muddled up in my head, I can't speak— [*Laughing.*] We arrived at the auction, Deriganoff was already there. Leonid Andreyevitch had only fifteen thousand and Deriganoff right off bids thirty over and above indebtedness. I see how things are, I match him with forty thousand. He forty-five. I fifty-five. That is to say he raises it by fives, I by tens.— So it ended. Over and above the indebtedness, I bid up to ninety thousand, it was knocked down to me. The cherry orchard is mine now. Mine! [*Guffawing.*] My God, Lord, the cherry orchard is mine! Tell me I'm drunk, out of my head, that I'm imagining all this— [*Stamps his feet.*] Don't laugh at me! If only my father and grandfather could rise from their graves and see this whole business, see how their Yermolay, beaten, half-illiterate Yermolay, who used to run around barefoot in winter, how that very

Yermolay has bought an estate that nothing in the world can beat. I bought the estate where grandfather and father were slaves, where you wouldn't even let me in the kitchen. I am asleep, it's only some dream of mine, it only seems so to me— That's nothing but the fruit of your imagination, covered with the darkness of the unknown— [*Picking up the keys, with a gentle smile.*] She threw down the keys, wants to show she is not mistress any more— [*Jingling the keys.*] Well, it's all the same. [*The orchestra is heard tuning up.*] Hey, musicians, play, I want to hear you! Come on, everybody, and see how Yermolay Lopahin will swing the axe in the cherry orchard, how the trees will fall to the ground! We are going to build villas and our grandsons and great-grandsons will see a new life here.— Music, play! [*The music is playing.* LYUBOFF ANDREYEVNA *has sunk into a chair, crying bitterly.* LOPAHIN *reproachfully.*] Why, then, didn't you listen to me? My poor dear, it can't be undone now. [*With tears.*] Oh, if this could all be over soon, if somehow our awkward, unhappy life would be changed!

PISHTCHIK. [*Taking him by the arm, in a low voice.*] She is crying. Come on in the ballroom, let her be by herself— Come on— [*Taking him by the arm and leading him into the ballroom.*]

LOPAHIN. What's the matter? Music, there, play up! [*Sarcastically.*] Everything is to be as I want it! Here comes the new squire, the owner of the cherry orchard. [*Quite accidentally, he bumps into the little table, and very nearly upsets the candelabra.*] I can pay for everything!

[*Goes out with* PISHTCHIK. *There is nobody left either*

in the ballroom or the drawing-room but LYUBOFF ANDRE-
YEVNA, *who sits all huddled up and crying bitterly. The
music plays softly.* ANYA *and* TROFIMOFF *enter hurriedly.*
ANYA *comes up to her mother and kneels in front of her.*
TROFIMOFF *remains at the ballroom door.*]

ANYA. Mama——! Mama, you are crying? My dear, kind,
good Mama, my beautiful, I love you——I bless you. The
cherry orchard is sold, it's not ours any more, that's true,
true; but don't cry, Mama, you've your life still left you,
you've your good, pure heart ahead of you—— Come with
me, come on, darling, away from here, come on—— We will
plant a new orchard, finer than this one, you'll see it,
you'll understand; and joy, quiet, deep joy will sink into
your heart, like the sun at evening, and you'll smile,
Mama! Come, darling, come on!

CURTAIN

ACT FOUR

ACT FOUR

The same setting as in Act I. There are neither curtains on the windows nor are there any pictures on the walls. Only a little furniture remains piled up in one corner as if for sale. A sense of emptiness is felt. Near the outer door, at the rear of the stage, is a pile of suitcases, travelling bags, and so on. The door on the Left is open, and through it VARYA'S *and* ANYA'S *voices are heard.* LOPAHIN *is standing waiting.* YASHA *is holding a tray with glasses of champagne. In the hall* EPIHODOFF *is tying up a box, off-stage at the rear there is a hum. It is the peasants who have come to say good-bye.* GAYEFF'S *voice: "Thanks, brothers, thank you."*

YASHA. The simple folk have come to say good-bye. I am of the opinion, Yermolay Alexeyevitch, that the people are kind enough but don't understand anything.

[*The hum subsides.* LYUBOFF ANDREYEVNA *enters through the hall with* GAYEFF; *she is not crying, but is pale, her face quivers, she is not able to speak.*]

GAYEFF. You gave them your purse, Lyuba. Mustn't do that! Mustn't do that!

LYUBOFF ANDREYEVNA. I couldn't help it! I couldn't help it!

[BOTH *go out.*]

75

LOPAHIN. [*Calling through the door after them.*] Please, I humbly beg you! A little glass at parting. I didn't think to bring some from town, and at the station I found just one bottle. Please! [*A pause.*] Well, then, ladies and gentlemen! You don't want it? [*Moving away from the door.*] If I'd known that, I wouldn't have bought it. Well, then I won't drink any either. [YASHA *carefully sets the tray down on a chair.*] At least, you have some, Yasha.

YASHA. To those who are departing! Pleasant days to those who stay behind! [*Drinking.*] This champagne is not the real stuff, I can assure you.

LOPAHIN. Eight roubles a bottle. [*A pause.*] It's devilish cold in here.

YASHA. They didn't heat up today, we are leaving anyway. [*Laughing.*]

LOPAHIN. What are you laughing about?

YASHA. For joy.

LOPAHIN. Outside it's October, but it's sunny and still, like summer. Good for building. [*Looking at his watch, then through the door.*] Ladies and gentlemen, bear in mind we have forty-six minutes in all till train time! Which means you have to go to the station in twenty minutes. Hurry up a little.

TROFIMOFF. [*In an overcoat, entering from outside.*] Seems to me it is time to go. The carriages are ready. The devil knows where my rubbers are. They've disappeared. [*In the door.*] Anya, my rubbers are not here! I can't find them.

LOPAHIN. And I have to go to Harkoff. I'm going on the same train with you. I'm going to live in Harkoff all winter. I've been dilly-dallying along with you, I'm tired of doing nothing. I can't be without work, look, I don't know what to do with my hands here, see, they are dangling somehow, as if they didn't belong to me.

TROFIMOFF. We are leaving right away, and you'll set about your useful labors again.

LOPAHIN. Here, drink a glass.

TROFIMOFF. I shan't.

LOPAHIN. It's to Moscow now?

TROFIMOFF. Yes. I'll see them off to town, and tomorrow to Moscow.

LOPAHIN. Yes— Maybe the professors are not giving their lectures. I imagine they are waiting till you arrive.

TROFIMOFF. That's none of your business.

LOPAHIN. How many years is it you've been studying at the University?

TROFIMOFF. Think of something newer. This is old and flat. [*Looking for his rubbers.*] You know, perhaps, we shall not see each other again; therefore, permit me to give you one piece of advice at parting! Don't wave your arms! Cure yourself of that habit—of arm waving. And also of building summer cottages, figuring that the summer residents will in time become individual landowners; figuring like that is arm waving too— Just the same, however, I like you. You have delicate soft fingers like an artist, you have a delicate soft heart—

LOPAHIN. [*Embracing him.*] Good-bye, my dear boy. Thanks for everything. If you need it, take some money from me for the trip.

TROFIMOFF. Why should I? There's no need for it.
LOPAHIN. But you haven't any!

TROFIMOFF. I have. Thank you. I got some for a translation. Here it is in my pocket. [*Anxiously.*] But my rubbers are gone.

VARYA. [*From another room.*] Take your nasty things! [*Throws a pair of rubbers on to the stage.*]

TROFIMOFF. But what are you angry about, Varya? Hm.— Why, these are not my rubbers.

LOPAHIN. In the spring I planted twenty-seven hundred acres of poppies and now I've made forty thousand clear. And when my poppies were in bloom, what a picture it was! So look, as I say, I've made forty thousand, which means I'm offering you a loan because I can afford to. Why turn up your nose? I'm a peasant—I speak straight out.

TROFIMOFF. Your father was a peasant, mine—an apothecary—and from that absolutely nothing follows. [LOPAHIN *takes out his wallet.*] Leave it alone, leave it alone— If you gave me two hundred thousand even, I wouldn't take it. I am a free man. And everything that you all value so highly and dearly, both rich man and beggars, has not the slightest power over me, it's like a mere feather floating in the air. I can get along without you, I can pass you by, I am strong and proud. Humanity is moving toward the loftiest truth, toward the loftiest happiness that is possible on earth and I am in the front ranks.

LOPAHIN. Will you get there?

TROFIMOFF. I'll get there. [*A pause.*] I'll get there, or I'll show the others the way to get there.

[*In the distance is heard the sound of an axe on a tree.*]

LOPAHIN. Well, good-bye, my dear boy. It's time to go. We turn up our noses at one another, but life keeps on passing. When I work a long time without stopping, my thoughts are clearer, and it seems as if I, too, know what I exist for, and, brother, how many people are there in Russia who exist, nobody knows for what! Well, all the same, it's not that that keeps things circulating. Leonid Andreyevitch, they say, has accepted a position—he'll be in a bank, six thousand a year—the only thing is he won't stay there, he's very lazy—

ANYA. [*In the doorway.*] Mama begs of you until she's gone, not to cut down the orchard.

TROFIMOFF. Honestly, haven't you enough tact to— [*Goes out through the hall.*]

LOPAHIN. Right away, right away— What people, really!

[*Goes out after him.*]

ANYA. Has Fiers been sent to the hospital?

YASHA. I told them to this morning. They must have sent him.

ANYA. [*To* EPIHODOFF, *who is passing through the room.*]
Semyon Panteleyevitch, please inquire whether or not they
have taken Fiers to the hospital.

YASHA. [*Offended.*] This morning, I told Egor. Why ask
ten times over!

EPIHODOFF. The venerable Fiers, according to my con-
clusive opinion, is not worth mending, he ought to join
his forefathers. And I can only envy him. [*Putting a suitcase on a hat-box and crushing it.*] Well, there you are,
of course. I knew it. [*Goes out.*]

YASHA. [*Mockingly.*] Twenty-two misfortunes—

VARYA. [*On the other side of the door.*] Have they taken
Fiers to the hospital?

ANYA. They have.

VARYA. Then why didn't they take the letter to the
doctor?

ANYA. We must send it on after them— [*Goes out.*]

VARYA. [*From the next room.*] Where is Yasha? Tell him
his mother has come, she wants to say good-bye to him.

YASHA. [*Waving his hand.*] They merely try my patience.

[DUNYASHA *has been busying herself with the luggage;
now when* YASHA *is left alone, she goes up to him.*]

DUNYASHA. If you'd only look at me once, Yasha. You are
going away—leaving me— [*Crying and throwing herself
on his neck.*]

YASHA. Why are you crying? [*Drinking champagne.*] In

six days I'll be in Paris again. Tomorrow we will board
the express train and dash off out of sight; somehow, I
can't believe it. *Vive la France!* It doesn't suit me here—
I can't live here— Can't help that. I've seen enough ignorance—enough for me. [*Drinking champagne.*] Why do
you cry? Behave yourself properly, then you won't be
crying.

DUNYASHA. [*Powdering her face, looking into a small
mirror.*] Send me a letter from Paris. I loved you, Yasha,
you know, loved you so! I am a tender creature, Yasha!
YASHA. They are coming here. [*Bustling about near the
suitcases, humming low.*]

[LYUBOFF ANDREYEVNA, GAYEFF, ANYA *and* CHARLOTTA
IVANOVNA *enter.*]

GAYEFF. We should be going. There is very little time left.
[*Looking at* YASHA.] Who is it smells like herring!

LYUBOFF ANDREYEVNA. In about ten minutes let's be in the
carriage— [*Glancing around the room.*] Good-bye, dear
house, old Grandfather. Winter will pass, spring will be
here, but you won't be here any longer, they'll tear you
down. How much these walls have seen! [*Kissing her
daughter warmly.*] My treasure, you are beaming, your
eyes are dancing like two diamonds. Are you happy?
Very?

ANYA. Very! It's the beginning of a new life, Mama!

GAYEFF. [*Gaily.*] Yes, indeed, everything is fine now.
Before the sale of the cherry orchard, we all were
troubled, distressed, and then when the question was

settled definitely, irrevocably, we all calmed down and were even cheerful— I'm a bank official. I am a financier now— Yellow ball into the side pocket, anyway, Lyuba, you look better, no doubt about that.

LYUBOFF ANDREYEVNA. Yes. My nerves are better, that's true. [*They hand her hat and coat.*] I sleep well. Carry out my things, Yasha. It's time. [*To* ANYA.] My little girl, we shall see each other again soon— I am going to Paris, I shall live there on the money your Yaroslavl grandmother sent for the purchase of the estate—long live Grandmother! But that money won't last long.

ANYA. Mama, you'll come back soon, soon— Isn't that so? I'll prepare myself, pass the examination at high school, and then I'll work, I will help you. We'll read all sorts of books together. Mama, isn't that so? [*Kissing her mother's hands.*] We'll read in the autumn evenings, read lots of books, and a new, wonderful world will open up before us— [*Day-dreaming.*] Mama, do come—

LYUBOFF ANDREYEVNA. I'll come, my precious. [*Embracing her daughter.*]

[LOPAHIN *enters with* CHARLOTTA *who is softly humming a song.*]

GAYEFF. Lucky Charlotta: she's singing!

CHARLOTTA. [*Taking a bundle that looks like a baby wrapped up.*] My baby, bye, bye— [*A baby's cry is heard: Ooah, ooah—!*] Hush, my darling, my dear little boy. [*Ooah, ooah—!*] I am so sorry for you! [*Throwing the bundle back.*] Will you please find me a position? I cannot go on like this.

LOPAHIN. We will find something, Charlotta Ivanovna, don't worry.

GAYEFF. Everybody is dropping us, Varya is going away. —All of a sudden we are not needed.

CHARLOTTA. I have no place in town to live. I must go away. [*Humming.*] It's all the same—

[PISHTCHIK *enters.*]

LOPAHIN. The freak of nature—!

PISHTCHIK. [*Out of breath.*] Ugh, let me catch my breath—I'm exhausted— My honored friends— Give me some water—

GAYEFF. After money, I suppose? This humble servant will flee from sin! [*Goes out.*]

PISHTCHIK. It's a long time since I was here— Most beautiful lady— [*To* LOPAHIN.] You here—? Glad to see you —a man of the greatest intellect— Here— Take it— [*Giving* LOPAHIN *some money.*] Four hundred roubles— That leaves eight hundred and forty I still owe you—

LOPAHIN. [*With astonishment, shrugging his shoulders.*] I must be dreaming. But where did you get it?

PISHTCHIK. Wait—I'm hot— Most extraordinary event. Some Englishmen came and found on my land some kind of white clay— [*To* LYUBOFF ANDREYEVNA.] And four hundred for you—Beautiful lady—Wonderful lady— [*Handing over the money.*] The rest later. [*Taking a drink of water.*] Just now a young man was saying on the train that some great philosopher recommends jumping off roofs—"Jump!" he says, and "therein lies the whole problem." [*With astonishment.*] You don't say! Water! LOPAHIN. And what Englishmen were they?

PISHTCHIK. I leased them the parcel of land with the clay for twenty-four years— And now, excuse me, I haven't time—I must run along—I'm going to Znoykoff's—To Kardamonoff's— I owe everybody— [*Drinking.*] I wish you well—I'll drop in on Thursday—

LYUBOFF ANDREYEVNA. We are moving to town right away, and tomorrow I'm going abroad—

PISHTCHIK. What? [*Alarmed.*] Why to town? That's why I see furniture—Suitcases— Well, no matter— [*Tearfully.*] No matter— Men of the greatest minds—those Englishmen— No matter— Good luck—God will help you. —No matter— Everything in this world comes to an end —[*Kissing* LYUBOFF ANDREYEVNA's *hand.*] And should the report reach you that my end has come, think of that well-known horse and say: "There was once on earth a so and so—Semyonoff Pishtchik— The kingdom of Heaven be his." Most remarkable weather—yes— [*Going out greatly disconcerted, but immediately returning and speaking from the door.*] Dashenka sends her greetings!

[*Goes out.*]

LYUBOFF ANDREYEVNA. And now we can go. I am leaving with two worries. First, that Fiers is sick. [*Glancing at her watch.*] We still have five minutes—

ANYA. Mama, Fiers has already been sent to the hospital. Yasha sent him off this morning.

LYUBOFF ANDREYEVNA. My second worry—is Varya. She is used to getting up early and working, and now without any work she is like a fish out of water. She has grown thin, pale and cries all the time, poor thing— [*A pause.*] You know this, Yermolay Alexeyevitch: I dreamed—of marrying her to you. And there was every sign of your getting married. [*Whispering to* ANYA, *who beckons to* CHARLOTTA, *both go out.*] She loves you, you are fond of her, and I don't know, don't know why it is you seem to avoid each other—I don't understand it!

LOPAHIN. I don't understand it either, I must confess. It's all strange somehow— If there's still time, I am ready right now even— Let's finish it up—and basta, but without you I feel I won't propose.

LYUBOFF ANDREYEVNA. But that's excellent. Surely it takes only a minute. I'll call her at once.

LOPAHIN. And to fit the occasion there's the champagne. [*Looking at the glasses.*] Empty, somebody has already drunk them. [YASHA *coughs.*] That's what's called lapping it up—

LYUBOFF ANDREYEVNA. [*Vivaciously.*] Splendid! We'll go out— Yasha, allez! I'll call her— [*Through the door.*] Varya, drop everything and come here. Come on! [*Goes out with* YASHA.]

LOPAHIN. [*Looking at his watch.*] Yes—

[*A pause. Behind the door you hear smothered laughter, whispering, finally* VARYA *enters.*]

VARYA. [*Looking at the luggage a long time.*] That's strange, I just can't find it—

LOPAHIN. What are you looking for?

VARYA. I packed it myself and don't remember where.

[*A pause.*]

LOPAHIN. Where do you expect to go now, Varvara Mikhailovna?

VARYA. I? To Regulin's. I agreed to go there to look after the house— As a sort of housekeeper.

LOPAHIN. That's in Yashnevo? It's nigh on to seventy miles. [*A pause.*] And here ends life in this house—
VARYA. [*Examining the luggage.*] But where is it? Either I put it in the trunk, perhaps— Yes, life in this house is ended—it won't be any more—

LOPAHIN. And I am going to Harkoff now—By the next train. I've a lot to do. And I am leaving Epihodoff—on the ground here—I've hired him.

VARYA. Well!

LOPAHIN. Last year at this time it had already been snowing, if you remember, and now it's quiet, it's sunny. It's only that it's cold, about three degrees of frost.

VARYA. I haven't noticed. [*A pause.*] And besides our thermometer is broken— [*A pause. A voice from the yard through the door.*] Yermolay Alexeyevitch—

LOPAHIN. [*As if he had been expecting this call for a long time.*] This minute! [*Goes out quickly.*]

[VARYA, *sitting on the floor, putting her head on a bundle of clothes, sobs quietly. The door opens,* LYUBOFF ANDREYEVNA *enters cautiously.*]

VARYA. [*She is not crying any longer, and has wiped her eyes.*] Yes, it's time, Mama. I can get to Regulin's today, if we are just not too late for the train— [*Through the door.*] Anya, put your things on! [ANYA, *then* GAYEFF *and* CHARLOTTA IVANOVNA *enter.* GAYEFF *has on a warm overcoat, with a hood. The* SERVANTS *gather, also the* DRIVERS. EPIHODOFF *busies himself with the luggage.*] Now we can be on our way.

ANYA. [*Joyfully.*] On our way!

GAYEFF. My friends, my dear, kind friends! Leaving this house forever, can I remain silent, can I restrain myself from expressing, as we say, farewell, those feelings that fill now my whole being—

ANYA. [*Beseechingly.*] Uncle!

VARYA. Dear Uncle, don't!

GAYEFF. [*Dejectedly.*] Bank the yellow into the side pocket— I am silent—

[TROFIMOFF *and then* LOPAHIN *enter.*]

TROFIMOFF. Well, ladies and gentlemen, it's time to go!

LOPAHIN. Epihodoff, my coat!

LYUBOFF ANDREYEVNA. I'll sit here just a minute more. It's as if I had never seen before what the walls in this house are like, what kind of ceilings, and now I look at them greedily, with such tender love—

GAYEFF. I remember when I was six years old, on Trinity Day, I sat in this window and watched my father going to Church—

LYUBOFF ANDREYEVNA. Are all the things taken out?

LOPAHIN. Everything, I think. [*Putting on his overcoat. To* EPIHODOFF.] Epihodoff, you see that everything is in order.

EPIHODOFF. [*Talking in a hoarse voice.*] Don't worry, Yermolay Alexeyevitch!

LOPAHIN. Why is your voice like that?

EPIHODOFF. Just drank some water, swallowed something.

YASHA. [*With contempt.*] The ignorance—

LYUBOFF ANDREYEVNA. We are going and there won't be a soul left here—

LOPAHIN. Till spring.

VARYA. [*She pulls an umbrella out from a bundle, it looks as if she were going to hit someone;* LOPAHIN *pretends to be frightened.*] What do you, what do you— I never thought of it.

TROFIMOFF. Ladies and gentlemen, let's get in the carriages— It's time! The train is coming any minute.

VARYA. Petya, here they are, your rubbers, by the suitcase. [*Tearfully.*] And how dirty yours are, how old—!

TROFIMOFF. [*Putting on the rubbers.*] Let's go, ladies and gentlemen!

GAYEFF. [*Greatly embarrassed, afraid he will cry.*] The train— The station— Cross into the side, combination off the white into the corner—

LYUBOFF ANDREYEVNA. Let's go!

LOPAHIN. Everybody here? Nobody there? [*Locking the side-door on the Left.*] Things are stored here, it must be locked up, let's go!

ANYA. Good-bye, house! Good-bye, the old life!
TROFIMOFF. Long live the new life!

[*Goes out with* ANYA. VARYA *casts a glance around the room and, without hurrying, goes out.* YASHA *and* CHARLOTTA, *with her dog, go out.*]

LOPAHIN. And so, till spring. Out, ladies and gentlemen— Till we meet. [*Goes out.*]

[LYUBOFF ANDREYEVNA *and* GAYEFF *are left alone. As if they had been waiting for this, they throw themselves on one another's necks sobbing, but smothering their sobs as if afraid of being heard.*]

GAYEFF. [*In despair.*] My sister, my sister—

LYUBOFF ANDREYEVNA. Oh, my dear, my lovely, beautiful orchard! My life, my youth, my happiness, good-bye!

ANYA. [ANYA'S *voice, gaily, appealingly.*] Mama—!

TROFIMOFF. [TROFIMOFF'S *voice, gaily, excitedly.*] Aaooch!

LYUBOFF ANDREYEVNA. For the last time, just to look at the walls, at the window— My dear mother used to love to walk around in this room—

GAYEFF. My sister, my sister—!

ANYA. [ANYA'S *voice.*] Mama—!

TROFIMOFF. [TROFIMOFF'S *voice.*] Aaooch—!

LYUBOFF ANDREYEVNA. We are   oming! [*They go out.*]

[*The stage is empty. You hear the keys locking all the doors, then the carriages drive off. It grows quiet. In the silence you hear the dull thud of an axe on a tree, a lonely, mournful sound. Footsteps are heard. From the door on the right* FIERS *appears. He is dressed as usual, in a jacket and a white waistcoat, slippers on his feet. He is ill.*]

FIERS. [*Going to the door and trying the knob.*] Locked. They've gone. [*Sitting down on the sofa.*] They forgot about me— No matter— I'll sit here awhile— And Leonid Andreyevitch, for sure, didn't put on his fur coat, he went off with his topcoat— [*Sighing anxiously.*] And I didn't see to it— The young saplings! [*He mutters something that cannot be understood.*] Life has gone by, as if I hadn't lived at all— [*Lying down.*] I'll lie down awhile— You haven't got any strength, nothing is left, nothing— Ach, you—good-for-nothing— [*He lies still.*]

[*There is a far-off sound as if out of the sky, the sound of a snapped string, dying away, sad. A stillness falls, and there is only the thud of an axe on a tree, far away in the orchard.*]

CURTAIN

NOTES

THE CHERRY ORCHARD

Page 3 line 22—"My father, who is at rest." This is precisely what Lopahin says. He is a peasant and would not say in the European fashion "My dear Father," which would mean the father was dead.

Page 4 line 21—Epihodoff is a variant on ignorance and pomposity, his speeches have, therefore, to be understood accordingly. The translation here, then, is entirely faithful, and the actor should indicate that he knows Epihodoff is what he is. Otherwise the translation will seem wrong.

Page 12 line 18—Podyovka is a Russian coat high at the neck with buttons following a figure seven, tight at the waist and flaring out to just below the knees. Sharovary are full-cut pants that tuck into high boots.

Page 13 line 3—Patchouli is a very cheap perfume, low grade, smelly.

Page 13 line 24—"Kissing Fiers"—this of course means on the cheek or the forehead.

Page 22 line 5—"Oh, no, no, God bless you, Mama!" Here the meaning is that her mother is to preserved from speaking so. If advisable, you could substitute "Oh, no, don't say that, Mama," or "Oh, no, Mama, you mustn't." The actor's tone if right can express the idea without changing Chekhov's words.

"You little cucumber!" The cucumber in Eastern and semi-Eastern countries is eaten as apples are with us, or peaches. If the effect causes the wrong amusement in the audience, I should advise the actor to say instead: "You little peach!" The effect is the thing to be sought here.

Page 43 line 10—"Free and easy with the servants." What Chekhov really says is that they are careless about using the "thou" with the servants. Since our language does not have the "you" and "thou" distinctions—the *tutoyer* of the French, the *lei* and *voi* of the Italians, it seems wrong to waste the valuable dramatic time value merely to keep the exact line. The decision as to that can be settled in each producer's mind.

Page 47 line 1—"Achmelia." A joke on the word Ophelia. If not clear to the audience it is not worth preserving. Translators try "Oh, feel me," etc. The thing to do in production is to keep the joke if plausible, if not, merely to say Ophelia.

Page 76 line 9—"Pleasant days to those who stay behind." Chekhov's line is merely "A pleasant stay." This can be used if the actor turns to those who are going to stay and makes the toast. A point to be noted here is that it would be better to keep Chekhov's line, "A pleasant stay," if the stage business can be right to give the idea. It should be noted, too, that there are two toasts, distinctly. Chekhov's stage directions do not indicate this clearly. The fact that Yasha makes two toasts can be made by the actor playing the part to be an element in Yasha's pretentious affectation and self-complacency and impudence. Yasha can be made a very important rôle in the play. His impertinence is a measure more or less, in terms of the vulgar mind, of the decline of the family. All the rôles in this play are notable and Yasha is one of the best. Most actors that I have seen, all of them in fact, play the rôle as merely as saucy valet. In Chekhov's plays, I may say, there is nothing ever that is "merely."

As to the title one may notice a certain confusion among critics and translations as to the word "orchard." We are sometimes told that the title should be *The Cherry Garden;* and now and then in a translation the word "garden" gets into the lines instead of "orchard." This comes from the fact that in Russian there is no such word as "orchard." The word is "garden"—an apple garden for example, which makes no sense in English. They have a word for a vegetable garden—"ogorod"—and no descriptive adjective is needed to make that clear. "Cherry garden" in English suggests a Japanese conception. The orchard in Chekhov's play is a commercial proposition, like a cornfield or a vineyard.

Finally, it ought to be suggested that actors playing the rôles in *The Cherry Orchard* should not conceive them as older than they are. It must be remembered that in *War and Peace* Tolstoy speaks of the old countess as worn out with child bearing and as sallow et cetera, she was fifty.

CAPTIVE
Jan Buttram

Comedy / 2m, 1f / Interior

A hilarious take on a father/daughter relationship, this off beat comedy combines foreign intrigue with down home philosophy. Sally Pound flees a bad marriage in New York and arrives at her parent's home in Texas hoping to borrow money from her brother to pay a debt to gangsters incurred by her husband. Her elderly parents are supposed to be vacationing in Israel, but she is greeted with a shotgun aimed by her irascible father who has been left home because of a minor car accident and is not at all happy to see her. When a news report indicates that Sally's mother may have been taken captive in the Middle East, Sally's hard-nosed brother insists that she keep father home until they receive definite word, and only then will he loan Sally the money. Sally fails to keep father in the dark, and he plans a rescue while she finds she is increasingly unable to skirt the painful truths of her life. The ornery father and his loveable but slightly-dysfunctional daughter come to a meeting of hearts and minds and solve both their problems.

OTHER TITLES AVAILABLE FROM SAMUEL FRENCH

TAKE HER, SHE'S MINE
Phoebe and Henry Ephron

Comedy / 11m, 6f / Various Sets
Art Carney and Phyllis Thaxter played the Broadway roles of parents of two typical American girls enroute to college. The story is based on the wild and wooly experiences the authors had with their daughters, Nora Ephron and Delia Ephron, themselves now well known writers. The phases of a girl's life are cause for enjoyment except to fearful fathers. Through the first two years, the authors tell us, college girls are frightfully sophisticated about all departments of human life. Then they pass into the "liberal" period of causes and humanitarianism, and some into the intellectual lethargy of beatniksville. Finally, they start to think seriously of their lives as grown ups. It's an experience in growing up, as much for the parents as for the girls.

"A warming comedy. A delightful play about parents vs kids. It's loaded with laughs. It's going to be a smash hit."
– New York Mirror